AF405823

Object Lessons

A Parris Island Memoir

© 2023, Terry Dwyer

Preface

I have contemplated writing this account of my time at Parris Island ever since reading the novel written by Edwin McDowell back in 1980 about Marine Corps boot camp. While his was fiction, I decided that nonfiction was more appropriate and that truth sometimes really is stranger than fiction. This excerpt from the book *U.S. Marines In Vietnam: The War That Would Not End, 1971-1973* by Charles Melson sets the backdrop of my account much more eloquently than I ever could have:

"By July 1971, less than 500 U.S. Marines, mostly advisors, communicators, and supporting arms specialists remained in Vietnam. It was thought at the time that the success of "Vietnamization" of the war would lessen even this small number, as it was hoped that the South Vietnamese could continue fighting successfully. This hope vanished in spring

1972, dashed by a full-scale North Vietnamese Army invasion. The renewed combat saw the U.S. Marines return once more to Southeast Asia in a continuation of the war that now seemed to have no end. The fighting proceeded into the fall, and only ceased with the signing of peace accords in Paris in January 1973."

I had kept in my head so many events and jotted down so many notes over the years from that period in 1972 that it wasn't hard to overlay them with a calendar from that timeframe. For those events that I might be off on actual dates by a couple days, they're close enough to keep the retelling relevant and meaningful. Obviously, the conversations recounted here are my best recollection and intended to convey the gist and intent of said events and conversations. If someone wants to question the accuracy or veracity of my account, so be it. I haven't exaggerated any of my recollections or manufactured them out of thin air.

To the extent that I have avoided naming specific guys in my platoon, I've done so out of a sense of courtesy. I haven't changed the names of any of our

Drill Instructors simply because, in retrospect, those men volunteered for and accepted an unbelievable task at an unbelievable time and they deserve recognition for serving as Marine Corps Drill Instructors. I know that there are a lot of Marines who made it through Parris Island and believe that their Drill Instructors had little integrity or honor. Whether our platoon was the exception or the rule is irrelevant; there is a message here in these pages. What that message says depends on the reader's perspective.

To those who would say that this is more of the "same old, same old", that this story has been told a thousand times, and if one didn't go through Parris Island, there is no personal frame of reference for the reader, especially 50 years later - ok, maybe you're right. But it's my story, it did happen, and it meant and still means something to me.

Chapter 1

The Beginning

In my senior year of high school in the winter and spring of 1972, I was pretty much fed up with school. At my mother's prodding, I had submitted my application for the Naval Academy and my "safety" option was an ROTC scholarship to the University of Florida. Frankly, I didn't really know what either one of those involved except that I was committing myself to four years of a free college education in exchange for another six years in the military as a commissioned officer. I pursued only those two opportunities.

Two of my high school classmates had applied to the Air Force Academy for reasons that I didn't quite understand. Both guys were members of the High School Cross Country team and decided that the AFA was a good next step for them. As the three of us compared notes over the winter months, they were pretty fired up to get to Colorado Springs and get started. I wasn't so fired up to get to Annapolis and get started but I didn't even begin to have the money to go to a college or university if it wasn't a service academy or an ROTC program.

The Naval Academy had experienced a recent cheating scandal and had dismissed a number of midshipmen so I figured that the reduced Midshipman population would result in a higher quota of incoming freshmen and improve my chances of getting accepted. Although U.S involvement was beginning to wind down in the Vietnam War, many newspapers were still reporting casualties on a daily basis and the number of in-country troops there, while being reduced pretty quickly from the 1968 high of 530,000, was still around 155,000 by the end of 1971. This entered into my calculus that a lot of high school seniors, either on their own or at the behest of their parents, would be less inclined to pursue those avenues for higher education.

Also entering into my calculus was my brother's experience with the military draft lottery. In 1970, he had drawn a number around 350 so his chances of being drafted that year were somewhere between slim and none. The next year's lottery left him with a number somewhere around 50 which practically guaranteed that he would be drafted with a 99% chance of being drafted into the Army. Rightly so, he wasn't going to wait for that day to come so he enlisted in the Air Force.

As I watched those events unfold, I had the classic attitude of a lot of young men at that time: the Vietnam War was a far-off event on the other side of the world and at the age of 17, death or injury on a battlefield simply didn't register with me.

In the spring of 1972, a phone call informed me that a retired Navy vice admiral in the Orlando area was ready to interview me as soon as possible. I soon discovered that was the next step on the path to an appointment to Annapolis. One person even told me that if the Admiral was impressed enough with me and my qualifications, my application would be forwarded on to the U.S. Representative for our district, and that I would really have to screw up not to make it all the way to Annapolis. Then I also discovered that the only available majors at the Naval Academy at the time were in Math, Science, and Engineering. Uggghhh...

By my senior year, I had decided that I really did not care for Science or Math so that pretty much cinched it for me. Cancelling the interview wasn't an option since I would never hear the end of it from my mother so the next best choice for me was to give the Admiral a visual memory of me that would be really hard to overcome. I showed up for my interview wearing blue jeans, sneakers, and my Budweiser T shirt.

I was respectful to the Admiral and answered all of his questions as best I could. But my attire clearly sent the intended message and caught his attention because when I got home that night from my after-school job, my mother harangued me about my choice of clothes for the interview and told me that the Admiral had called her almost immediately after the interview to tell her that her son obviously wasn't taking this whole process seriously. Because everything else looked pretty good on my application, he told her, he would be willing to give me another chance for the interview. My reply? Nope. I was done with the Naval Academy.

Around the same time, I was doing so well in my High School German classes to the point that my teacher wanted to submit my name for the annual State High School German Language competition in Coral Gables. I didn't know it at the time, but she had submitted my name for the highest competition category and the winner would be declared the Florida State High School German Language student of the year. I went into the competition with a more subdued version of my usual "fuck you, watch me" attitude and won. On the morning announcements over the P.A. system when we got back to school the following Monday, my teacher announced to the entire school that I had won that award. I remember thinking to myself, "Wow...maybe I've found what I want to do after High School."

That pretty much sealed my decision to continue with my German language studies. A little more research on my part uncovered the possibility of going to the Foreign Language Center at the Defense Language Institute. Given my good grades and my recent award, the only remaining key was to be a member of the military.

That's when my thoughts turned to the Marine Corps. I had met an older cousin at my grandmother's house when I was 8 years old and he was stationed as a Marine at the Mayport Naval Base in Jacksonville, Florida. I remember seeing him in his Summer Service A uniform, admiring his appearance and wanting to look like that when I was older. A few years later, our family was invited to his wedding right after he had graduated from Officer Candidate School. At the wedding, he was wearing the Dress Whites of a Marine Corps officer and some of his comrades were there in their dress blue uniforms. To this day, I still remember how great they all looked and how much I wanted my own set of dress blues one day.

Those memories came back to me in tremendous detail in the spring of my Senior Year. I decided that the Defense Language Institute was my goal and the quickest path there was to enlist in the Marine Corps. Vietnam? Mehhh... I'd worry about that when the time came. Remembering my cousin, an officer in the Marine Corps, I knew that being an officer had its perks. "What could be worse?" I thought. I knew that I just wanted to get the hell out of Orlando.

As luck would have it, about a week later, an envelope arrived in the mail with a bunch of forms. They were the papers I needed to fill out and mail back to whatever government agency that was running the ROTC selection so they could process my selection for the program. I looked at them and I looked at them some more. All I had to do was sign on the dotted line and that ROTC scholarship effectively was mine. I didn't feel like waiting four years to get to my end goal of the Defense Language Institute so I tore up the papers, threw them in the trash, and didn't tell a soul what I did.

I knew what my next step would be so I waited a few weeks. Sometime in June after the school year had ended, I went to the local Marine Corps recruiting station and signed up for a four-year enlistment. There were three sessions with the Marine Staff NCO at the recruiting station. The first one was the initial paperwork routine, telling him what I was interested in and what my skills were.

Since I had won the state-wide award for high school German language students, I had this dream of going to the Defense Language Institute and getting posted somewhere that would let me use my skills as a fairly fluent German language interpreter. Back then, one could sign up for two, three, or four years. I signed up for four years.

When the recruiter told me that I needed to pass a typing test for this general MOS field, my immediate thought was "WTF?" I asked him why and he said it was just part of the qualification process for the field that I was interested in.

"It's not a problem", he said. "We'll take care of that."

He called me a couple days later to let me know that I had passed the typing test that I DID NOT take and that I needed to come in to sign a few more papers. After signing them, I came home and told my mother that I had signed up with the Marine Corps for four years. She was unhappy to the point that she cried pretty much for the rest of that night.

After a few more steps along the way, I boarded a Greyhound bus on September 18, 1972, headed for the

AFEES Station in Jacksonville, Florida. On the next day, along with a few dozen other young guys, I stood there in a room and was sworn into the Marine Corps. We then boarded another Greyhound bus. Next stop, Parris Island.

There was still a lot going on at that time. "Vietnamization" wasn't going especially well and there were still regular updates in newspapers of Americans killed or wounded in action. Walter Cronkite was still on a roll four years after he publicly questioned the country's involvement on an episode of the CBS Evening News.

Overlaid on the most recent events there was a combination of recent race riots a few years before and an economy doing pretty poorly. President Nixon had instituted wage and price controls but to a high school senior like me, that didn't mean squat. However, that would pop up later in a most unusual way.

I don't remember the exact time but it was somewhere around midnight when we passed through the gates and arrived at what looked like a World War II-vintage building. The bus doors opened and a

Marine stood outside the bus yelling at us to get off the bus and put our feet on the yellow footprints in the pavement.

After a minute or so, we were all standing on the yellow footprints in front of the Receiving building and I remember glancing quickly around me to survey the situation. Even on surface appearance, we were a true amalgamation of society's young men. That was jarringly brought home to me along with other revelations multiple times before I left the island three months later.

After a few more instructions/orders, we were herded into a World War II vintage Quonset hut with lots of well-worn mattresses lying side by side on the floor. We were told to pick one out, lie down on it and get some sleep because we were going to need it. Before I fell asleep, the old TV show "Gomer Pyle, USMC", with all the Quonset huts featured in that show, came to mind and I immediately thought, "So this is what it looks like. This isn't so bad so far..."

Boy, was I wrong.

Chapter 2

Day One

The lights came on sometime around 4 am. They weren't joking before – it would have been nice to get a couple more hours sleep.

We formed up outside again in the dark on the yellow footprints and were sort of marched over to the mess hall but the commands were more like "hippity ho, herd go" and "hippity hop, herd stop". There were a couple platoons in their green utilities already queued up outside the mess hall about to enter. A few of those guys glanced over at us and a Drill Instructor promptly barked at them, "Head and eyes straight ahead, ladies, unless you'd like to join them!"

After a really brief breakfast, we went back to the mattress room where we were allowed to sleep until daylight. Then it was back out to the yellow footprints and we were off to get haircuts. I remember waiting in line watching one guy with shoulder length hair being shorn by the barber in what seemed thirty seconds. There were eighty of us and only three or four barbers but the whole process took only minutes.

Then it was off to yet another Quonset hut where we were each given one set of skivvies (a set of boxer briefs and a T shirt). We were told to empty our pockets as they explained that all individual possessions were about to be stored in individually named containers. Everything: wallets, money, ID's, keys. Everything.

We also received our first Marine Corps issue. One of my new platoon mates questioned the size of the boots he was given by the supply NCO despite the fact that they had just instructed us in the other room to write down on a form our arm length, waist size, and shoe size. The reply was "take your fucking boots and move on." Obviously, questioning the judgment or decisions of those in authority here was not viewed well. I soon learned that the reactions rarely ended there.

We stuffed our issue into the sea bags they gave us at the front of the line. Then it was back out to the yellow footprints. The staff NCO from the Quonset hut was still with us and he herded us over to another building where we filled out forms for what seemed an eternity because we went from there straight over to the mess hall for lunch.

There were a few more stops to the infirmary for shots and a quick physical exam, another Quonset hut to change into our new "utilities" and place our civilian clothes in a rather large cloth sack for storage until we left the island,. Then we were herded back to yet another Quonset hut with racks and mattresses to leave our sea bags filled with our new issue.

A new NCO appeared in the squad bay and curtly told us to pick a mattress. At that point, another NCO appeared and was introduced as our Senior Drill Instructor, SSgt Allen. The first NCO then told us we had a couple minutes to go pee in the head because we were not going to be allowed out of our racks during the night.

It had been hours since the last time we were allowed a pee-break and I really needed to relieve myself. There was only one problem – 72 guys and three urinals. I stood in line for about 30 seconds and decided that I wouldn't make it in time while waiting in line and that the showers looked good enough to pee in. I hurried into the shower room which had about 8 or 10 shower heads on two of the walls facing each other, took aim at a drain and drained my bladder as quickly as I could. I was followed by about another 10 guys who had also realized that they weren't going to make it to a urinal in the allotted two minutes.

Back out in the squad bay, as we stood on line we could hear the NCO rousting the remaining guys out of the head. Apparently, a lot of them didn't get to pee so I felt lucky that at least I was able to pee in the shower and not in my rack that night. But I wasn't that lucky.

One of my new platoon mates yelled out to the Senior Drill Instructor that some of us had peed in the showers. The Senior Drill Instructor barked out, "Who pissed in my showers? Get your asses up here NOW!"

I hesitated only for a couple seconds before I hurried up to the front of the squad bay in front of the Drill instructor. I didn't say a word. I didn't have to.

"You pissed in my showers?"

"Yes sir."

He pulled a chair over to him and barked "Drop your trou and grab the back of the chair!"

I complied and he removed his black leather Senior Drill Instructor belt from his waist. After about 5 stinging lashes across my buttocks which were covered only by my skivvies, I was allowed to pull up my trousers and get back on line.

No one else had come forward so he bellowed again, "Who else pissed in my showers? I know there were more of you!"

A few came forward and received the same punishment. I wasn't keeping track because I was pretty far down the line of racks and too focused on my aching buttocks and my embarrassment.

Then it was time to get in the rack before they turned the lights out but not before the barracks NCO warned us not to try to piss into our canteens during the night because the offenders might end up having to drink their piss the next day. As I lay there, I realized that this had to have happened with every other platoon who had spent the night in this squad bay. There were always going to be a few like me who violated the rules of good behavior and paid for it. I wondered for a few days if the Drill Instructor would hold this against me down the road. I quickly discovered that my offense was minor and was to serve as an object lesson to everyone including me: **if you do something stupid or against the rules, be prepared for the consequences.**

Once punishment had been meted out, everyone moved on until there were further transgressions or outright failures to comply by the same idiot. Then the punishment escalated from there. Boy, did it escalate!

Chapter 3

Forming

We had already been told that our drill instructors were going to "pick us up" the next day. After breakfast, we headed back to the Quonset hut to get our sea bags and stand on line for further orders. The wait couldn't have been more than a minute because we were then ordered outside onto the yellow footprints with our sea bags where the drill instructors were waiting. And then it began.

Our destination was 1st Battalion barracks, about a mile away. We were basically a group of humans being herded across the streets and over the parade deck to an H-shaped three-story brick building. I remember thinking, "thank God, we're here" and once again I was wrong. The drill instructors ran us at a pretty fast walking pace around the entire barracks building not once, not twice, but three times. There were a couple guys who dropped out and the drill instructors were all over them, yelling at them to get back with the rest of the platoon.

Then it was up the stairwell to the third floor and in the door to the squad bay. Again, it was 1972 and this place looked pretty brand new to me. There were two yellow lines running down the length of the squad bay, each one a couple feet away from a row of double bunk bed racks on either side of the squad bay. The drill instructors yelled at us to drop our sea bags in front of a rack, any rack, and put our feet on the yellow line.

From that point on through the evening with only a quick break for dinner at the mess hall, they had us inventory every piece of our issue and mark every piece of clothing with name stamps right then and there that we made a few minutes before. If anyone was missing anything, they were to shout out that they didn't have it and the drill instructors made note of it.

As the evening wore on, there was a small group of guys at one end of the squad bay who kept calling out that they were missing something. The drill instructors obviously had run into this before because they figured out that someone in the immediate area was stealing items from other guys nearby. It took only about a minute for the Drill Instructors to discover the jerk who was doing this and then they were all over him, yelling and haranguing him, asking him what the hell was his problem and why was he doing this.

Then the jerk took a swing at one of the drill instructors and that was it. They tackled him and hauled him off to the other end of the squad bay into the bathroom area (AKA "the head") and that was the last we all saw of him. Again, another object lesson: **If you disrupt the flow of platoon activity or, God forbid, take a swing at a Drill Instructor, there will be dire consequences.**

We finished inventorying and marking all our gear and then it was time for showers and shaving. No more lessons tonight and no more incidents. I lay there in my bed wondering what the hell I had done by enlisting in the Marine Corps and realized that by then it was too late. I was going to have to tough it out.

The next day started with breakfast – oops, morning chow - and back to the concrete platform right outside the barracks building which was right next to the chow hall. There we learned for the first time (but not the last time) how to assemble in platoon formation. There were four lines (aka "ranks") with anywhere from 15 to 20 guys in each rank, depending on what stage of boot camp the platoon was in. Over the course of three months, the number of recruits in a given platoon would vary anywhere from 60 to 80 depending on a number of factors, including recruit drops and adds.

Proper distance from the guy in front of you was determined by extending your left arm and fingers until you touched the back of his left shoulder. Proper distance from the guy to your left was determined by extending your left arm and fingers while turning your head to the right. It was the responsibility of the person to your left to inch over to your fingers until your fingers barely touched him.

If you were at the far right of that rank, you extended your left arm but kept your head facing forward. If you were at the far left of that rank, you kept your arms at your side but still turned your head to the right and inched over to the guy on your right until your right shoulder barely touched his outstretched fingers. A Drill Instructor then gave the command "Cover!" at which point everyone in the second, third and fourth ranks were to align as closely as possible behind the guy in the first rank. At that point we were considered to be in proper platoon formation.

From there it was the basics of close order drill while remaining stationary: right face, left face, about face, and so on. Actual marching while in formation was quite another experience that often included punishment PT on the spot.

Then we were off to the base armory where we were each issued an M-14 rifle, then back to the barracks and up to the squad bay where we all locked our rifles to the ends of our bunk racks facing the windows.

Before the beginning of the Forming Phase, everyone filled out paperwork to open up a bank account in the on-base bank and have pay deposited there during boot camp. After graduation, recruits could then withdraw the savings and change their "direct deposit" to any bank account of their choosing.

Everyone then went through medical, dental, and eye exams. No one was allowed to wear contact lenses during boot camp although contact lenses were still pretty much a novelty among eyeglass wearers.

If someone required glasses to reach 20/20 vision, they were given military-issue glasses with thick, hard-plastic black frames and hard-plastic lenses. No one was allowed to wear civilian glasses either after receiving the military-issued glasses. However, if they determined that glasses weren't needed to see, the recruit did not have to wear them. After graduation, one could wear their civilian glasses again, as long as they conformed to military dress and appearance regulations.

During the next few days, we were also introduced to the basic marching aspects of close order drill without our rifles. Looking back, I could imagine that civilians probably never considered the effort and practice required for approximately 70 guys to march in formation, remaining in step with the rest of the platoon, while still maintaining the proper distance between themselves and the guys to their front, right, and left. But as we would all learn, learning to march with that kind of precision would require weeks of practice.

And then there was close order drill with our rifles. It wasn't complex to learn but normal human behavior emerged during this part of training. Some of the guys would tilt their heads to the left when executing the "right-shoulder-arms" movement or tilt their heads to the right when executing the "left-shoulder-arms" movement. This was to avoid hitting themselves in the head when bringing the rifle up alongside their heads from any other position.

Some of the guys tilted their heads a little – some guys tilted their heads a lot. It didn't matter to the Drill Instructors how little the tilts were. We were supposed to execute these moves with NO tilts of the head. Period. The fore arm was also supposed to run exactly parallel to the ground while the upper arm was to be exactly alongside the upper body with the angle of the rifle roughly at 45 degrees to the body every time. Period.

The Drill Instructors had an interesting way of
having us practice rifle drills. Occasionally, they would
have each of us stand back-to-back with another guy
in spaced out platoon formation where, if we executed
rifle movements correctly, the likelihood of hitting the
guy in back of any of us with our rifles was remote. If
any of us were inclined to tilt our heads while
performing any of the movements that involved
bringing the rifle up to our shoulders or down from
our shoulders, we would bang our rifle barrels into the
heads of the guys standing back-to-back with us
because our rifles wouldn't have the necessary
clearance to avoid hitting the other guy in the head.
After much practice (and head banging), everyone
pretty much learned how to perform these movements
without tilting their heads. Another object lesson:
Little things are big things.

There was also "port arms", "sling arms", "order
arms", "trail arms", "parade rest", "inspection arms"...
Needless to say, these all required constant practice
and repetition for the rest of our time at Parris Island.
Trying to get 70-odd guys to perform each movement
properly and precisely in unison while in formation

was a lot easier said than done as we would soon find out in the first phase and third phase drill competitions. But rifle drill was one of the basic training regimens to instill discipline and precision in a platoon that would carry over even to combat situations as the Drill Instructors would tell us over and over.

Another topic to learn and remember was the list of eleven General Orders. In 1972, the wording was only slightly different from today's version:

1. **Take charge of this post and all government property in view.** This included the authority to stop and question any rank who seeks to pass through that post's area.

2. **Walk my post in a military manner, keeping always on the alert and observing everything that takes place within sight or hearing.** This one was and still is especially important since standing guard in a combat zone could be a life or death situation.

3. **Report all violations of orders I am instructed to enforce.** This included the

maintenance of the post's written log to keep track of all events that occurred while on watch.

4. **To repeat all calls from posts more distant from the guardhouse than my own.**

5. **Quit my post only when properly relieved.**

6. **To receive, obey, and pass on to the sentry who relieves me, all orders from the Commanding Officer, Officer of the Day, Officers, and Non-Commissioned Officers of the guard only.** This included any special orders given during that duty day to the relief sentry.

7. **Talk to no one except in the line of duty. It is all business when on duty.**

8. **Give the alarm in case of fire or disorder.** This included calling for backup if necessary.

9. **To call the Corporal of the Guard in any case not covered by instructions.**

10. **Salute all officers and all colors and standards not cased.** Regular military courtesy always applied in these situations.

11.   **Be especially watchful at night and during the time for challenging, to challenge all persons on or near my post, and to allow no one to pass without proper authority.**

It may sound like something that didn't matter that much, but in all branches of the military, it was and still is a big deal even though the general orders vary slightly from branch to branch. And it soon became obvious to everyone in our platoon that memorizing the General Orders would help avoid "physical reminders" to memorize them.

Fortunately, these were part of the contents of the Marine Corps Handbook that everyone received as part of the original issue. The handbook was approximately 4x6 inches and about three fourths of an inch thick with the pages attached to a metal spiral binding at the top. It contained most information that we needed to learn and memorize and was apparently designed to fit in a recruit's back pocket. There were also numerous blank pages at the end of the handbook on which we could write additional information during classes or other inside instructional sessions although we were usually instructed to bring it along only for those occasions.

Another physical aspect of boot camp that I'm sure most of us in the platoon didn't factor in was the coastal climate, especially for that time of the year towards the end of summer. While many of us had grown up in that kind of hot and humid summer weather, it was still pretty oppressive spending much of the time outdoors. For recruits going through Parris Island during June, July, and August, everyone was issued "chrome domes", helmets painted in a somewhat reflective silver color that were shaped just like combat helmets. The Drill Instructors informed us that we would do just fine wearing our olive-drab-colored utility covers. Thank God that we didn't have to keep them on during regular daily PT.

It's also worth noting that in 1972, the standard color for utilities was olive drab, or "OD". The camouflage, or "camo" look, did not come in until some years later. Likewise, the standard combat boots were straight black unlike the tan-colored boots with really thick cotton material on the lace-ups covering the ankles. Neither change would have made a damned difference back then and, looks-wise, we probably wouldn't have cared less.

About one week into the forming phase, we were allowed to write letters to parents/wives/girlfriends informing them that we were here at Parris Island, we were doing fine, and we could receive letters at the return address on the envelope, but "nothing else, please". No details, no "get me out of here!" pleas, just that we were doing fine and there would be more to come. Shortly after those first letters went out, mail started coming in.

More importantly, "care packages" started arriving. These packages could be anything: clothes, toiletries, food. Clothes were packed back up and put in storage with the original clothes we were wearing when we first arrived on the Island, to be taken home after graduation by the recruit who received the clothes. Toiletries supposedly were packed up and also put in storage for retrieval at graduation time although I don't recall anyone mentioning anything about them still being there at graduation time.

Food was another story. It was usually baked goods which supposedly would survive the U.S. Mail system for weeks if properly wrapped. Sometimes they were properly wrapped and sometimes they weren't. It wasn't hard to notice either way but it didn't matter.

Any food deliveries were opened by the addressee (who was called up to the front of the squad bay in front of everyone) and were usually dumped promptly in the trash can for all to see with very few exceptions. Sometimes we were reminded of this prohibition but still, the exceptions were very rare – except for one very entertaining incident which would play out in Third Phase with unexpected results.

Bedtime was also referred to as "square away time" which was supposedly free time for everyone. In reality, it almost always involved the three S's (shit, shower, and shave), then back to our foot lockers where, if there was any time left, one could scrawl out a letter back home to someone.

This was also when we learned to shine our recently issued combat boots and dress shoes. The adjective "spit shined" was a misnomer. It always involved a cloth, Kiwi black shoe polish, and a little water from the canteen on the end of the rack. Since this was in the era before they issued dress shoes using corfam material requiring next to no shining effort, dress shoes had all-leather uppers with next to no sheen to them. It took a while to build up a layer of polish on the shoes that would produce a pretty good shine. It only took about a week to figure out that shining our combat boots was merely to ensure that they would last and that the leather would not crack during boot camp. A few guys did experience cracked leather on their boots but for the most part, the occasional shine effort helped everyone's boots last.

Then a Drill Instructor would come out of the duty hut, a smallish room with a desk and a few racks with mattresses, and bark out that we all had one minute before inspection. Inspection started with everyone pulling their foot lockers out away from the racks and perpendicular to the yellow line in front of each of the two rows of racks. Everyone stood on the end of their respective foot lockers in their skivvies and "shower shoes" (flip flops), dress shoes right alongside us on the squad bay floor, and extended their hands out with palms down, forearms parallel with the deck (the floor) and upper arms alongside the torso. Assuming this stance sooner rather than later was always a good idea, as a few of us would eventually find out the hard way.

It should also be noted that part of our original issue upon arrival at Parris Island included plenty of pairs of skivvies and we were expected to put on a new pair every night after taking showers. The skivvies consisted of white t-shirts and white boxer-style bottoms. As someone who had never worn a pair of boxers in his life, only briefs or "tighty whities" up to that point, I was a little uncomfortable at first wearing them. After a few days, I resigned myself to the requirement to wear them for the rest of boot camp.

White cotton laundry bags had been handed out as part of our original issue, each of them respectively marked by each of us during that first night in the squad bay, and the Drill Instructors were unfailing in their collection of those laundry bags containing dirty utilities, skivvies, and anything else used or soiled during a given training day, every few days in the morning. In turn, that same night the laundry bags were returned to us with everything in them washed and dried. As part of "square away time" on those nights, everyone put their clean laundry back in their foot lockers. Frankly, I could never recall a single day or night that any of us did not have clean utilities and skivvies to start out the day. Someone might think that it wasn't that big a deal or that the Drill Instructors adhered to that schedule because of the consequences of failure on their part. I, for one, was impressed that that practice continued up until the day before graduation.

Inspection included checking the closeness of our shave results and checking for any cuts or bruises that required immediate attention. In one of my moments of idle thought, I was impressed with both of these aspects. One involved attention to detail, which they always harped on, and the other was to ensure that no one had any obvious physical issues. One could always make the argument that the Drill Instructors were just covering their asses but, as I would learn later, they also were not insensitive to someone having physical problems.

Inspection completed, the command would come: "Prepare to mount!" Everyone scrambled to push foot lockers back to their previous positions at the foot of their respective bunk racks and then stood at attention on either side of the bunk.

"Mount!"

Everyone climbed on to their bunks, lying on top of the sheets and wool blanket at attention.

At that point, depending on the moment and the individual Drill Instructor, we would recite our General Orders, sing the Marine Corps Hymn, or recite something else in unison before the Drill Instructor would bark, "Lights Out!" The lights went out and we could get under the covers if we wanted to. Many of us chose to sleep on top of our sheets and covers because after getting up the next morning, everyone had to make sure that their respective racks were properly made, including hospital corners on the bed sheets and covers, and bed blankets pulled appropriately tight enough that a Drill Instructor could bounce a coin on the top of the blanket.

There were a few lessons in the beginning on making our racks and after the first couple weeks, this became one of the less important aspects of boot camp since it was obviously easier to learn than most other tasks.

We also learned that first night in the squad bay while we were marking our gear that the piece of clothing we put on our heads every morning when we went outside was called a "cover". Not a hat or a cap. **A COVER**. It was another easy lesson to learn but there were a couple guys who slipped up after a few days and called it a cap when addressing one of the Drill Instructors.

There were other terms to learn as well. The floor was the deck. A wall was a bulkhead. The bathroom was the head. A doorway was a portal. For almost all of us in the platoon, this environment was what we chose when we enlisted in the Marine Corps whether we knew it or not. Some of us, like me, thought we knew what we had signed up for but the actual experience went far beyond anything we had been told up to that point, and we were only at the beginning of boot camp.

Every day after morning chow, we would form on the concrete platform outside our barracks building and march over to the PT field for Physical Training. Early on in Forming, we all took the initial Physical Fitness Test. The PFT consisted of three simple parts:

pull-ups, sit-ups, and the three mile run. A perfect score of 300 could be achieved with 20 pull-ups, 80 sit-ups (crunches) in two minutes, and a three mile run in 18 minutes or less. There were also minimums – I passed the 3 mile run and the pull-ups but didn't get the minimum sit-ups in 2 minutes. There were about another dozen guys who also didn't pass every part of the PFT. Luckily, there was no punishment for failing the initial PFT but everyone soon realized what they needed to focus on to pass the final PFT and get off the Island.

Regular morning PT routines varied but usually included bends-and-thrusts (an exaggerated version of a push-up), windmills, sit-ups, and the three mile run, with the run always at the end of PT. While running in formation, our Drill Instructors would run alongside our platoon during the three mile run, chanting verses that we were to repeat. While these verses were intended to help maintain cadence and timing while running in formation, the words were pretty colorful.

"I know a girl in New Orleans…. She kisses sailors and blows Marines."

"I don't know but I've been told… Eskimo pussy is mighty cold."

"Left, Right, left…Left right left…"

There were other equally spicy cadence phrases, all of which brought a little variation and entertainment to an otherwise hum-drum, occasionally painful, three mile run.

The run was also the ultimate yardstick to measure the fitness of every guy in the platoon as we discovered on the first day of PT. Despite the warnings from our Drill Instructors, about a dozen guys dropped back behind the platoon as we ran in formation. Even I felt a few times like I wouldn't be able to keep up but the fear of the consequences forced me to keep in pace with the rest of the platoon.

The "run drops" paid the penalty after we got back to the squad bay by being herded into the head where they were "counseled". Those of us closest to the head heard a lot of yelling and thuds that sounded like people bouncing off the walls in there. It only lasted for a couple minutes and then the "run drops" came back out and got back on line with the rest of us. It didn't require an explanation from the Drill

Instructors for the rest of us to realize what had just happened. **Another object lesson: Give it your all or there will be consequences.**

After a few more days, repeat "run drops" then got to experience the "motivational platoon". After morning chow, they were pulled out of formation and told to stand off to the side while the rest of the platoon marched off to the PT field. Later in the afternoon, the platoon marched back to the barracks where we saw the same group of guys standing there, staring straight ahead, covered head to toe in mud with all-metal mock rifles the same size and length of our M-14s at order arms. That was everyone's introduction to "one day mote", a half-day experience that included crawling 500 yards through a mud pit and being forced to watch a combat film showing Marines in a fire fight with the enemy.

If there was any better way to be "scared straight" during boot camp, I couldn't think of it and to this day, I still can't think of one. After graduation, my mother gave me a bunch of photos from an issue of a magazine published during my time at Parris Island that included an article complete with numerous photos. One picture was of a member of our platoon looking up at the photographer while crawling through mud carrying his mock metal M-14. Decades later, looking at his eyes as he looked up at the photographer while crawling on his belly through the mud, it reminded me of a huge object lesson: **Screw up once and there will be consequences. Screw up again on the same task and the consequences will be worse - guaranteed**.

Drill instructors nowadays are not supposed to use excessive profanity, nor are they allowed to physically touch a recruit other than for safety reasons, such as on the weapon range, or to correct the recruit's stance or uniform. So how do they maintain discipline? In the other services, it may be push-ups, or possibly some running. In the Marine Corps, a recruit gets "quarterdecked" although that term was not used back then. For lack of a better term, quarterdecking today is a euphemism for IT, or Incentive Training, and is administered to some or all of the platoon to get everyone's attention after some screw-up.

Every recruit platoon had three drill instructors. When present, the Senior Drill Instructor gave the majority of the commands and orders while the other two Drill Instructors singled out those who appeared to have performance problems (physical or behavioral), and administered physical discipline, now known officially as IT (Incentive Training).

IT now consists of prescribed exercises (supposedly a maximum of five minutes outside in "the pit," no maximum inside the squad bay). Exercises that one could expect include "bends and thrusts", leg lifts, side lunges, side straddle hops (AKA jumping jacks), and push-ups – LOTS of push-ups. In 1972, bends and thrusts were actually "bends and whoopies" - exaggerated bends and thrusts, in which the individual bent over, placed his palms flat on the ground, kicked his legs out, let his ass sag almost to the ground, brought the legs back up with his palms still on the ground and then stood up. Needless to say, "bends and whoopies" took a greater toll on the body than bends and thrusts.

Today, drill instructors use a combination of individual and group IT sessions to keep the platoon on its toes. Back then, IPT was just the beginning and was often skipped in favor of "direct physical contact" between the Drill Instructors and the offending recruit. The offense could be as minor as slapping a sand flea off one's face while outside in formation but was usually something like not obeying an order quickly enough or, worse yet, being a "run drop".

Punishment often involved a punch to the solar plexus. It didn't cause any harm to the recruit on the receiving end of the punch but it did literally knock the wind out of the recruit and cause a little pain at the same time. I rarely saw the Senior Drill Instructor hit one of us, which we all figured out after a while because one of them had to be the final arbiter of harsher punishment.

Harsher punishment ranged from extended IPT to banishment for one to three days at a "motivational platoon". "One day mote" was a more common punishment for those who continually failed to stay in formation for the three mile run at the end of every morning's PT session or, worse yet, was an obvious "run drop". "Three day mote" was for those who continually failed to stay in formation, continually failed to follow orders, did not have a weight problem, and usually had been through one day mote.

Talking back to the Drill Instructors or showing a lack of respect toward them would also quickly earn a visit to the motivational platoon. Committing these offenses on a regular basis even after a trip to the motivational platoon meant that the recruit had discipline problems and resulted in even harsher punishment called "CCP".

CCP was the acronym for the Correctional Custody Platoon, the last stop before outright discharge from the Marine Corps. CCP punishment usually lasted for a week followed by reassignment to a new platoon and spending an extra week on the island. Worse yet, the Drill Instructors at the offender's new platoon after his week in CCP knew of the recruit's time in CCP which made it all the more difficult for that recruit to continue boot camp.

During Forming, the Drill Instructors arranged us in formation according to descending height, the tallest recruits being at the front of every column and the shortest ones at the rear. There were four "columns" and the person at the head of each column wasn't necessarily the tallest but someone deemed by the Drill Instructors to have some potential as a "squad leader", at first primarily determined by their performance during PT and the three mile run. While not a good yardstick to use for a leadership position in the platoon, the Drill Instructors really had nothing else to go on at that point other than that.

They also picked one other guy to be the "guide". This person led the platoon in close order drills on the Parade Deck, was at the head of the formation when we marched to other locations on the Island, and was to carry the "guidon", starting in first phase, during the three mile run every morning toward the end of morning PT. The guidon was a wooden pole approximately seven feet long with a flag on the upper end with the platoon's number printed on it. During first and second phases, the numbers were in scarlet on a gold background. During third phase the colors were reversed with gold numbers on a scarlet background.

Toward the end of Forming and during the first week of First Phase, we were marched over to classrooms and were informed that we would be taking the GCT, or General Classification Test, which was the closest thing to a general IQ test in the Marine Corps. Then we were informed that we could take additional tests in specific subjects such as Math and foreign languages.

So the recruiting NCO back home was right, I thought. This was my opportunity to punch my ticket to the Defense Language Institute. And while I was at it, I decided to take the additional Math test since I figured this might give me a leg up on achieving my goal. It only took about a week or so for the ramifications of the test results to play out.

Our platoon was part of a series of four platoons, each numbering about 70 recruits. The Marines commanding each series included a series commander and a series Gunnery Sergeant. In our case, the series commander was a First Lieutenant who looked a little old to be a First Lieutenant. As it turned out, he was what they referred to as a Mustang, a commissioned officer who had previously been an enlisted Marine. We didn't see either one of them that much except for morning PT.

One thing we did notice early on was the surrounding environment that was Parris Island. The island was named for Colonel Alexander Parris, the public treasurer of the South Carolina colony in the early 18th century. Since 1915 it had been a Marine Corps Recruit Depot, eventually serving as one of two Recruit Depots for the Marine Corps, the other one being in San Diego.

Geographically, Parris Island was on the lower South Carolina coast line near the city of Beaufort. The area had classic southern coastal weather which meant that the heat and humidity was constant from April through October and especially oppressive during the summer months. For anyone who had not grown up in the south, it was a rude awakening to what was in store for the next three months during that time frame. Even for someone like me who had grown up in Florida, it was uncomfortable given the constant physical exertion required as part of boot camp.

During the summer months, recruits always wore white T-shirts under their long-sleeved utility shirts, or "blouses" as the Drill Instructors liked to call them.

During the summer months, the heavy cotton material of the utility uniforms, both trousers and blouses, caused everyone to sweat profusely, especially when outdoors during PT, close order drill, or running the obstacle course. Because of this, platoons often wore only their white T-shirts and even occasionally gym shorts during morning PT. Some platoons were issued light-weight helmets painted a dull grayish silver to reflect the sun, called "chrome domes", and they often wore these when practicing close order drill.

We were apparently past the peak of the summer heat and humidity so we weren't issued chrome domes but we did go through morning PT sometimes in just our T-shirts during those first couple weeks depending on the weather forecast. By the time November and December rolled around, the temperatures had dropped low enough that we were allowed to wear "field jackets" which were olive drab green in color like our utilities, again made of heavy cotton material, and were similar to windbreakers that one wore in civilian life. These field jackets were also issued to us shortly after we received our initial clothing issue and were collected at the end of boot camp in December a day or two before graduation.

Compounding the heat and humidity of the climate during the summer was the existence of sand fleas. They were actually the size of gnats and the stuff of legends and tall tales among Parris Island graduates. For platoons standing in formation ANYWHERE outside on the island, it only took a matter of seconds before these little bugs attacked in force. Sand flea bites would result in little red bumps on one's skin that would itch like crazy, but woe to the recruit who would slap at them when they tried to bite him. Early on during boot camp, the Drill Instructors warned us not to slap at them. Getting caught often resulted in some kind of punishment depending on where we were standing in formation at the time.

Out on the parade deck, the offender would occasionally be forced to stand off away from the formation while we practiced close order drill and then pay for his transgression after we returned to the squad bay, especially if he was a repeat offender. Over by the barracks, out of sight from any outside observers, sometimes it would be a punch to the solar plexus.

Only a couple times, and this was early on during the Forming, did the offender have to conduct a burial for the dead sand flea in front of the entire platoon. We all figured out pretty quickly that the burial was mostly intended as theater by the Drill Instructors but the lesson was not lost on us: **We told you not to slap at the sand fleas, you wasted platoon training time by doing this, and now you and the entire platoon will pay for your offense in some other way.**

Along the way during Forming, we also got used to the terms "Horrible fucking puke" and "Useless piece of shit". These were usually intended as attention getters and exclamation points when someone in the platoon didn't keep up with everyone else. By and large, though, our Drill Instructors did make the effort to ensure that we survived the heat and humidity of the Parris Island summer. We usually carried our water canteens on our web belts when outside the barracks and at various times during training were allowed to drink from them during extended periods out in the sun.

Because of the excessive sweating, the Drill Instructors made a point to the entire platoon, not once but a few times to drill home the point, that if any of us had not had a bowel movement in the previous seven days, we were to raise our hand and the Drill Instructors would give some kind of laxative to the recruit having problems taking a shit.

Early on, I had absorbed the lesson: **Keep your mouth shut, don't complain about anything, speak only when spoken to, and don't volunteer for a damn thing.**

So when the Drill Instructors warned us about excessive constipation, I had already gone close to a week without having a bowel movement despite my best efforts at straining to shit when I was on the toilet. T refused to speak up about my problem but the warning did motivate me to start drinking a lot more water to help my bowels. After another week of straining but still no bowel movement, I finally was able to shit. I also noticed that some blood came out with my stool and again decided that I would keep that problem to myself as well.

During the rest of boot camp, I developed a case of hemorrhoids as a result of my constipation problems at the beginning. Decades later, I still have those hemorrhoids as reminders of that period in boot camp although they are much more noticeable now and still occasionally bleed. Looking back now, would I have done it any differently back then? On balance? No. Getting off the island on schedule was goal one and I wasn't going to take ANY chances of delaying that outcome.

Since there were a few guys in the platoon that were obviously overweight (AKA "fat bodies") and struggling to keep up in morning PT and the three mile runs, the Drill Instructors did not ship them off to the "fat body" platoon if they determined that a recruit was really making the effort to keep up with everyone else. The "fat bodies" also had to weigh themselves on a small weight scale very few days that the Drill Instructors brought out from the duty hut.

Amazingly, at least to me, most of the overweight guys in the platoon dropped so much weight that by third phase, their weight loss was noticeable to everyone. At the same time, it was also noticeable that a few of the overweight guys were not successful and were shipped off to the fat body platoon after a few weeks.

There were lots of little lessons those first couple weeks, repeated over and over. One that was drilled, and occasionally beat, into us was that we were not to refer to ourselves using first-person or second-person pronouns when speaking to a Drill Instructor. A recruit was to **ALWAYS** refer to himself as the "the private", not "I". Similarly, a recruit was to always address a Drill Instructor, **ANY** Drill Instructor, as "the Drill Instructor", not "you".

Ninety-nine percent of the time, we all successfully complied with this directive. Occasionally, however, a recruit would forget and say "I" or "you". The first few occurrences were ALWAYS met with a Drill Instructor's punch to the solar plexus, accompanied by the Drill Instructor's sarcastic question to the offending recruit "I!? **EYE!?** You think you're an eye, you horrible fucking puke?" In the same vein, addressing the Drill Instructor as "you" drew a similarly sarcastic question, "You!? **EWE!?** You think I'm a female sheep, asshole??" also accompanied by a punch to the solar plexus.

Those first few incidents caused many wide-eyed "WTF??" looks among the rest of us and there were still a few more incidents over the next few weeks. After the initial shock of these occurrences wore off for most of us, subsequent screw-ups by someone who had forgotten this lesson were often met with rolled-eye expressions and even a few small smiles by many of us. After the first few weeks, though, that lesson had been completely ingrained in the entire platoon and there were no more screw-ups in that regard for the rest of our time on the Island.

A couple weeks and countless lessons later, the Forming phase was over and the hard stuff was about to come.

Chapter 4

First Phase

On Friday, October 9, Forming ended and First Phase began. At the outset, we did lose a couple guys to the fat body platoon. These guys were obviously overweight and, according to the Drill Instructors, consistently had problems with PT during Forming. They weren't discipline problems but part of making it through boot camp was physical fitness and these guys clearly didn't make the effort.

As a platoon, we could already see which members would likely be discipline problems down the road, usually because of their attitudes toward other guys in the platoon or the training regimen in general. Ironically, a couple of those "problem" guys were initially selected as squad leaders primarily because of their ability to perform well during PT and the three mile runs.

After the scores came in from the GCT tests we all took during forming, the Drill Instructors had a new yardstick to measure potential for success as a squad leader. In retrospect, they weren't too far off the mark although there was the occasional bad choice, such as the guy who scored well on the GCT and had a couple years of college under his belt. But then we were introduced to the Obstacle Course.

The Obstacle Course involved approximately 8 parts, none of which were particularly difficult but, taken together, could tax one's muscle strength and stamina especially depending on the time of day and what other activities came before it. The rope climb toward the end of the course almost always separated the physically fit from those out of shape. Each one of the ropes was tied to a metal ring attached to a wooden cross beam 25 or 30 feet up from the ground. The ropes themselves were a little over one inch in diameter, small enough for us to grasp it with both hands but also big enough to climb up to the top.

Unlike some movies or videos that some of us may have seen up to that point, the only logical method to climb the rope was to jump up from the ground, grasp the rope with both hands, wrap one's leg around the rope twice, and plant the foot of the other leg on top of the rope resting on the ankle of the first leg. After bracing oneself, the object was to move both hands up the rope as much as possible to get another firm grasp, move one's legs up the rope while keeping them in the same position, and repeat the process until one reached the ring and grasped it with one hand.

It seemed pretty simple and straightforward until some of us realized that upper body strength and overall body weight were the two biggest factors in successfully reaching that ring at the top of the rope. And since the rope climb came at the end of the course, the physical effort exerted up to that point took a toll on overall stamina as well as one's upper body strength. Needless to say, there were a few guys who didn't make it up to the metal ring.

Also during First Phase, we started pugil stick training and hand-to-hand close combat training. Pugil sticks were about 5 feet long with padded foam ends. The purpose of this training was to simulate hand-to-hand combat with one's rifle. In reality, these pugil sticks were unwieldy and allowed bigger, heavier recruits to whoop up on smaller opponents. It was obvious that the Drill Instructors kept this in mind because they would usually stop one-on-ones between larger guys and the smaller guys after about a minute. But if the two combatants were relatively evenly matched, they let them go at it until one of them took a couple shots to the head or was just obviously worn out from the exchange.

This became another metric for squad leader selection not because one had to win every pugil stick fight but how one held up during these encounters. I always gave it my best shot but fighting was never one of my best assets because I just didn't have the skill or aptitude. As a result, I got clobbered three times in a row in the pit, the last one being a pretty good whack to my head despite wearing a helmet as everyone always did. I popped right up after that third whack, a little dazed but ok to move out of the pit.

The winnowing process for squad leaders continued and then one day, one of the squad leaders screwed up. I was called up to the front of the platoon and told that I was the new squad leader for that column. I felt pretty good about that but figured that a part of my selection had to do with my scores on the tests. In brief conversations with other guys up to that point, I had noticed that a few guys had been in college. A couple of them had been designated squad leaders so it looked like the Drill Instructors placed some value on our test scores.

Another huge part of First phase consisted of classes and material covering Ranks, Insignia, General Orders, Chain of Command, and a host of other minutiae. Intuitively, I knew all of this was important but the repetitive nature of learning it was starting to be a bit much. It wasn't until later that I realized how important this aspect of boot camp was.

But every waking moment was spent on learning or practicing something. In afternoon classes, there was the occasional platoon member who dozed off simply because he was worn out at that point from everything else during the day. It was rare that we didn't see someone's head nodding but woe to the guy whose chin ended up on his chest and stayed there for any more than a couple seconds. One of the Drill Instructors would appear as if out of thin air and give the guy a good head slap. These head slaps continued throughout boot camp if for no other reason than to remind us (as the Drill Instructors often did) of another object lesson, tougher than most to learn: **Paying attention at all times could mean the difference between life and death in a combat situation**.

There were evenings in the head or elsewhere in the squad bay in which some of us were paired off, the high test scores guys like me with someone else in the platoon who was clearly not that bright but willing to bust his ass to make it through to graduation. Even if the more intelligent guys like me weren't good tutors, we knew what the drill instructors were looking for. It was repetition, repetition, repetition. Most of the guys we were paired with were appreciative of the help, as I soon noticed with the fellow I was always paired with. He was in the middle of the pack when it came to just about everything but he always tried his hardest and I occasionally reminded him that he always made the effort and that effort mattered the most.

Oftentimes, we would be standing on line in the squad bay when the Drill Instructors would walk up and down the squad bay, conducting ad-hoc question-and-answer sessions. And oftentimes, a recruit would not know the answer to a question posed by a Drill Instructor despite the constant repetition of reciting ranks, insignias, general orders and other minutiae. It wasn't unusual or rare – it was just being queried on some item out of the blue and a recruit would simply not remember.

When this happened, we had been directed early on to reply "Sir, the private doesn't remember." For example, when asked what was the fifth general order, someone might reply by starting with "Sir, the private's fifth general order is..." followed by a pregnant pause of a few seconds, followed by "Sir, the private doesn't remember his fifth general order."

Most of the time, the guy would get another chance to answer a different question but occasionally, if a lot of guys were forgetting answers up to that point, the Drill Instructor would become visibly unhappy and deliver a punch to the offending recruit. Did it motivate everyone to pay attention as questions were being posed up and down the line? I'd like to think so, but it was probably just demonstrating to everyone the need for more repetition.

There were even a few amusing moments like the time when we were all standing on line fielding random questions from the Drill Instructors on rank, insignia, and chain of command. As the Drill Instructors walked down the line firing off questions, one of the guys, Owens, was asked the name of the Series Gunnery Sergeant. Owens replied, "Sir, the Series Gun is Gunnery Sergeant Dawson!"

And just like that, the Drill Instructor and another one in the immediate vicinity descended upon Owens like a couple of hawks closing in for the kill. Those of us nearby watched out of the corners of our eyes as the two Drill Instructors landed a couple blows on him, yelling, "You don't refer to him as the Series Gun! You got that, asshole?"

We all knew that Owens gave the correct answer even if it came with a note of undue familiarity that even the Drill Instructors only occasionally used when referring to him. In retrospect, though, it was obvious that the punches were landed with next to no impact on Owens and he looked ok after his faux-pas. But that was another object lesson: **Keep everything formal and leave the terms of familiarity to the Drill Instructors when speaking with them about ANYTHING.**

Close order drill continued, sometimes on the parade deck and sometimes down a street or a clearing between streets. Out on the parade deck, we were able to see other platoons practicing close order drill nearby, including third phase platoons. We noticed the gap in proficiency between our platoon and those in third phase, and boy, what a difference! It didn't matter if they were the best in their series or the fourth best – they still looked impressive to us. During one of those moments, one of the Drill Instructors barked at us, "Look at them, ladies. That's how good you need to be."

One day, after apparently pissing off the Drill Instructors over something (which usually occurred every other day), we were marched around to the back of the barracks building. There was a one-lane paved path between the building and the marshy swamp that Parris Island was famous for. There were already numerous apocryphal tales about platoons being marched into the swamp and even one documented incident back in 1956 in which a Drill Instructor came back into the squad bay at night, rousted the platoon out of the racks and out to the marshes, and marched them into the swamp. Six recruits died as a result, the Drill Instructor was cashiered, and the story became a lesson for the Marine Corps on what not to do during recruit training.

Nonetheless, we proceeded to march into the marshes right next to that path but only about one third of the platoon ended up in the marsh before the Drill Instructors gave the "Halt" command. Nothing ever came of the incident but it didn't really matter. I saw no lesson in this experience and chalked this up to a moment of pettiness on the part of the Drill Instructors.

Another aspect of boot camp was the assignment early in first phase of two recruits to serve as "house mouse". As best we could tell, their responsibilities were admin tasks and general cleanup of the duty hut on a regular basis for the Drill Instructors. Apparently, they were told to never discuss what went on in the duty hut because we never heard any details. After a while, though, I think that everyone else could care less what duties they performed. We were all focused on getting off the island ASAP.

Later in First Phase, we were introduced to the confidence course. The course consisted of eleven obstacles, designed so that each obstacle was more physically challenging than the last. Today, the obstacles are: (1) Dirty name (2) Run, Jump & Swing (3) The Inclining Wall (4) The Confidence Climb (5) Monkey Bridge ("Monkey Ropes" when I was there) (6) The Tough One (7) Reverse Climb (8) Slide for Life (9) the Hand Walk (10) The Arm Stretcher, and (11) The Sky Scraper. While these names sound daunting, the course is designed so the entire platoon can run it in 45 minutes. It has been said that the Confidence Course was a great morale builder but I didn't think so. It just looked like another test of individual recruit abilities.

In any case, we were told to keep yelling as we progressed through the different obstacles. I understood why they told us to keep yelling, but everyone was more focused on getting through the course so the yelling died off at times. Apparently, the Drill Instructors noticed this when some of us were on the Monkey Ropes.

The Monkey Ropes were six sets of horizontally strung ropes between two wooden platforms both of which were 10 feet above the ground. One rope was six feet higher than the lower one and the object of the exercise was to place one's feet on the lower rope, grasp the upper rope and, using the ropes, sidle over a mud pit 10 feet below and be quick about it. On its own, the exercise wasn't difficult at all but after going through a few other obstacles already, yelling at the top of one's lungs while navigating the ropes didn't come readily to mind regardless of the command to do so.

So there I was, up on the ropes with five other guys, negotiating our way over the ropes to the other side, when the command came from below.

"Monkey ropes! Come to attention!"

Was that meant for us?

Again, the command: **"Monkey ropes! Come to attention!"**

We all paused for a split second, then stood straight up, arms at our sides. After another split second, we all tumbled into the mud pit. I wasn't happy about it because the previous group of guys going across the monkey ropes wasn't any more vocal than we were but it would be the first of a few more occasions that I thought were not fair. Another object lesson, only this one was more aligned with life in general: **Life isn't fair. Deal with it.**

Another memorable part of the confidence course was the Slide for Life. Everyone had to climb up an A-frame wooden ladder of sorts, stand on a wooden platform, reach out to grab an inch-thick rope that descended down at about a 20-degree angle for approximately 100 feet onto another wooden platform. As with other similar tests on the confidence and obstacle courses, there were multiple ropes, side by side, extending from that same wooden platform.

The objective was to pull yourself out on top of the rope, balancing your body on top of the rope with your arms draped over the rope in front of you and one leg draped over the rope in back. The other leg had to dangle down below you on the rope, which actually helped steady your body while on the rope.

Once in place, you pulled yourself down the rope to the platform at the other end, maintaining that same position. If you lost your balance and ended up hanging on to the rope from below with your hands and legs, or worse yet with just your hands, making it to the other end usually became a losing proposition. Someone rarely could get back on top of the rope and proceed on to the end because doing so required a level of upper body strength that 99% of us simply didn't have.

Every time that we ran the confidence course and came to the Slide for Life, the Drill Instructors would yell out to a few of us during that exercise "Rope 1! Reverse your position and continue down the rope!" This order meant that the guy on rope 1 had to swing his body around 180 degrees, ending up with his feet closer to the end of the rope.

At other times, the Drill Instructors would order one of the guys on one of the ropes to release his hands from the rope and let his arms dangle beneath the rope. After about 5 seconds, the guy was allowed to grip the rope with his hands and continue pulling himself down the rope to the other end. Obviously, the objective of this move was to maintain one's balance without the use of the hands gripping the rope. Also obviously, this move was easier to accomplish than the 180 degree turn but not by a whole lot depending on one's ability to balance oneself on the rope to begin with. With a group of 70-odd recruits going through the Slide for Life, it was inevitable that a few would not be able to maintain their balance on the ropes.

Complicating matters was the pit of three-feet-deep muddy water down on the ground below the ropes. The good news was that if you lost your grip and fell, you landed safely in the water below. The bad news was that you were usually soaked in muddy water when you climbed out of that pit and had to go around like that at least for the next few hours.

There were always a few out of every platoon that couldn't make it across and ended up in the pit, sometimes not of their own choice. The Slide for Life was at the end of the course and usually about mid-way through the whole exercise, there were guys waiting on the platform ready to go next after the guys in front of already on the ropes.

As always, some guys just weren't that fast in negotiating this particular exercise either because their sense of balance just wasn't that good or they actually were overly tentative in making it down the rope, often stopping while on the rope or ending up hanging on by their hands along the way.

Regardless, the Drill Instructors couldn't afford for these few to hold up the rest of the platoon and they would yell up to the slow pokes to stretch their arms out if they were on top of the rope in the correct position or to simply let go of the rope if they were hanging on by their hands.

In the first instance, those guys would usually lose their balance after a few seconds and fall into the water below. In the second instance, those guys obviously simply fell immediately into the water. The end result was the same.

As always, though, there was an object lesson with the Slide for Life: **Maintaining one's balance while doing anything in the field mattered.**

The inability to do so had not-so-good consequences.

Chapter 5

First Phase, Continued

As First Phase continued there were more tests, more chances to screw up, and a lot of us did not disappoint the Drill Instructors. About halfway through first phase, the Drill Instructors decided that a change in platoon guides was needed.

"Dwyer!"

I came up to the front of the squad bay and hollered, "Private Dwyer reporting as ordered, sir!"

"Dwyer, you're the new platoon guide."

"Aye aye, sir!"

I scurried back to my position on line and thought to myself, "Whoa! Now what?"

Being a platoon guide wasn't easy. You were always out front, whether you were practicing close order drill on the parade deck, running with the platoon guidon at port arms leading the platoon in the three mile run, or leading the platoon double-timing it to and from the confidence course. Although carrying the platoon guidon during the three mile run exhausted me at times, I was doing reasonably well or at least I thought so. Then one day, it happened.

We were on our way back to the barracks one day from the confidence course and I wasn't paying close attention to the direction that the Drill Instructor was headed. There was the usual path back to the barracks but halfway back, Sgt. Michel decided to take a different route. Shame on me for not paying attention but there I went down the usual route instead of following Sgt. Michel.

I immediately heard comments coming from the guys behind me and looked over to see that Sgt. Michel was already headed down a different path. Three of the squad leaders and about half of their squads had followed me but the fourth squad leader and most of his squad followed Michel. I immediately veered over to get the platoon back in formation behind Michel, but it was too late. Michel had already turned his head around to see a split platoon caused by my screw-up.

There are a lot of sins that one can commit while at Parris Island. I had just committed one of the cardinal sins: causing a split platoon. We were all back in formation behind Michel within a matter of seconds but I knew there would be a price to pay for my screw-up. As we ran along in formation, Michel looked over his shoulder and barked, "Guide, come see me when we get back to the barn!"

Back in the squad bay, we were all on line when Michel came out of the duty hut and said, almost in a low conversational tone, "Guide..."

Immediately, everyone in the platoon yelled, "Guide! Report to the Drill Instructor as ordered!"

This was SOP whenever one of the Drill Instructors wanted someone in the platoon to come to the front of the squad bay regardless of the reason. The Drill Instructor was usually standing right outside the duty hut so the person being summoned double-timed it up to the yellow footprints in front of the duty hut and yelled, "Sir, Private so-and-so reporting to the Drill Instructor as ordered!"

So I double-timed it up to the yellow footprints and announced in a loud voice, "Sir, Private Dwyer reporting to the Drill Instructor as ordered!"

Michel came over to my left side, placed his arm on my shoulders and said, again in a normal tone, "Dwyer, what the fuck were you thinking back there?"

"Sir, the private thought that the Drill Instructor was going back to the barn the usual way."

"You don't get to make those decisions. Got it?"

Almost immediately – OOOF! He punched me in the solar plexus. I bent over from having the wind knocked out of me and stood back up.

"Yessir!"

Then he took his arm off my shoulders and OOOF! He punched me in the solar plexus again, this time with a little more force. And this time, he knocked me back a couple steps off the footprints.

We had all learned early on that when one placed one's feet on the footprints, it didn't matter what came next. The rule was to keep one's feet on those footprints.

I stood there bent over for a second or two, trying to suck in my breath. Then I scrambled to get my feet back on the footprints.

"You're no longer the guide. Get your ass back on line."

Frankly, I can't remember who succeeded me as guide and I couldn't have cared less. The next day, I assumed my new place in the formation behind the shortest guys in the platoon. This was standard practice when someone was demoted from squad leader or guide. I also knew that I wouldn't stay at the rear of the formation because at my height, it would look odd having someone taller at the rear behind guys who were sometimes half a foot shorter when the platoon was in formation outside. Sure enough, the next day I was moved closer to the front of the formation with guys around the same height as me. And life went on.

Another part of first phase was learning to dis-assemble and re-assemble our M-14's. This made obvious sense since cleaning and maintaining one's weapon was a critical aspect of being a Marine. Most of the time, we only had to dis-assemble it into the three main parts: the receiver group, the stock, and the barrel group. Sometimes we would have to dis-assemble it further into smaller parts which occasionally would prove difficult for some guys in the platoon. Since everyone started dis-assembling their rifles at the same time, it wasn't hard to see the ones who were having a hard time with this task. The Drill Instructors weren't unnecessarily hard on those laggards and everyone eventually became somewhat familiar with the effort.

Probably about a week before the end of first phase, we were marched over to a Quonset hut and told that we were going to have our graduation pictures taken. Having been out in the South Carolina sun for weeks at that point, almost all of the Caucasian recruits had tanned faces which probably worked out well for the pictures.

In one room, there were dress blue blouses, midnight blue coats with standing collars. Normal dress blue blouses buttoned up on the front but these did not. Instead, they buttoned up from the back so some civilian helped put a reasonably fitted size on each of us and buttoned up the back of the blouse. The

Drill Instructors had already told us not to smile or smirk for the pictures and there would be only one shot taken so anyone who smiled did so at their own peril.

The proofs came back a few days later, were posted on the bulletin board outside the duty hut, and the Drill Instructors made good on their promise. Two guys were "counseled" in the head for smiling in their pictures.

A few days before the end of first phase, they held inspections for all four platoons in the series, conducted by the Series Gunnery Sergeant. On the night before, the Drill Instructors showed us how to apply liquid starch to one of our utility covers so that they looked angular with corners when placed on our heads. Right before the inspection, they conducted the drill competition among the four platoons in the series. Every platoon had been able to observe the other platoons as they practiced out on the parade deck and we knew who our toughest competition would be. Platoon 1004 was right up there with us in terms of precision of movements and maintaining proper spacing in formation.

Even the Senior Drill Instructor acknowledged that Platoon 1004 was pretty good. He had gone up against their Senior Drill Instructor, SSgt Haskell, in previous Drill Comps and told us that we couldn't afford any screw-ups competing against that platoon. Shortly after all four platoons completed their performances, the results were announced. Platoon 1004 won and we came in second. None of us was happy but as the Senior Drill Instructor had previously said, as long as we did our best, he was ok with the results. True to his word, he told us afterward that he thought it was a tie between us and the other platoon.

The next day, we moved out of our squad bay in the 1st Battalion barracks and marched over to the Weapons Battalion barracks by the Rifle Range for our next adventure.

Chapter 6

Snapping In at the Rifle Range

Monday, October 23.

We knew that the rifle range awaited us. As with everything else up to that point, we just didn't know what that entailed other than we were going to finally shoot live rounds from our M-14's at targets on a rifle range.

We marched over to the barracks area at the rifle range with our sea bags over our left shoulders and our rifles at sling arms over our right shoulders. Then up the stairwell to our new home for the next couple weeks. The barracks at the Weapons Battalion (as it was known) were definitely older than our squad bay in the 1st Battalion barracks during first phase but frankly, I couldn't have cared less. Getting unpacked and settled took very little time and then it was back outside to a grass field over by the rifle range itself where we were introduced to the concept and basics of "snapping in."

Most of the platoon's reaction to this "snapping in" work was "what the hell? You shoot the damn rifle and hopefully you qualify." There were three qualification levels – Marksman, Sharpshooter, and Expert. The maximum score was 250, a Marksman score was 190 to 210, Sharpshooter was 210 to 220, and Expert was 221 or higher.

We were also introduced to our Primary Marksmanship Instructor (PMI), Sergeant Richardson. During the introduction he announced that he went to high school in Orlando, Florida, and were there any of us from Orlando? Like a jackass, I raised my hand. Bad move on my part. **Another object lesson: don't volunteer any additional information unless you're prepared for the consequences**.

"What high school did you go to?"

"Colonial High School, sir."

"Colonial?? Us guys at Boone hated you fuckers!"

And that was the start of a two-week period that was part enlightening, part frightening, and occasionally entertaining.

We found out that day that we would be practicing snapping-in exercises that entire week and when we got into qualification week the following week, we realized why.

An M-14 fired a 7.62mm round which caused the rifle to kick like a small mule. That was also where we learned that the rifle strap served more than one purpose. The expectation was that, with the strap properly in place, after every shot, the muzzle of the rifle jumped up at most a few inches, and the shooter's firing position was to come back to rest at the same position as the previous shot with the muzzle pretty close to the same position as before. The sights on an M-14 weren't all that great but with the practice that came during the first three days of the following week, we would learn to adjust our sights accordingly.

Prior to the start of snapping in, we were each issued a shooting jacket to be worn over our utility shirts during the snapping in and live fire weeks.

These jackets did help because the padding around the top of each jacket in front of the shoulder area helped to absorb the recoil of the M-14 round being fired. It also helped that the daytime temperature there in late October in the late afternoon was a little cooler than it was a month earlier.

As part of these exercises, we learned how to wrap the strap around the same upper arm as our shooting eye and tighten it but not too much. The strap material was similar to that of our web belts and was adjustable like our web belts. We practiced the basic firing positions to be used the next week – sitting, prone, and standing. In the standing position, we were told to practice making "figure eights" while aiming at the target. For snapping in, we were told to focus on some distant object and practice the "figure eights" – the smaller the figure eight, the better.

We learned to contort our bodies in the sitting position not knowing that this was one of the key positions during qualification the next week. The repetition made a difference because each of us had to figure out where on our legs to place our elbows and forearms, and remember this for each shot when live fire started the next week. The placement of the strap on each person's upper arm while sitting also mattered because, once tightened around the upper arm, the strap would help bring the muzzle back to its previous position aimed at the target after the recoil of the previous shot. The placement of the rifle butt up snugly against the shooting shoulder made a difference because it lessened the recoil of the rifle. We would also discover during the next week the value of the shooting jackets.

For the prone position, the goal was to have one's arms and elbows in the most comfortable position but firmly in place, with the shooter's cheek resting on either the shooting hand or the rifle stock with the strap also properly tightened around the upper arm of the shooting hand and the rifle butt again snugly up against the shoulder. After snapping-in exercises every day (which seemed to go on for an eternity), there would be a little close order drill so we didn't forget what we had learned during the previous 5 weeks. The rote repetition of rank, insignia, and general orders also continued non-stop.

As always, there was PT every morning but this time, the DI's didn't push that hard on the PT or the three mile run. It didn't hurt either that all the constant run drops were no longer with the platoon and the occasional run drops had learned to gut it out.

One of the more memorable moments of that week was going through the chow line in the mess hall. That was our first direct exposure to the CCP – the Correctional Custody Platoon. We had been forewarned about the consequences of not following orders and not trying our hardest to comply with the regimen and the orders: counseling in the head, one day Mote, three day Mote, topped off with CCP before being summarily kicked out of the Corps. .

The recruits in the CCP platoon were hard cases – the ones who had decided that Parris Island and the Marine Corps wasn't for them. They weren't going to commit serious crimes. They probably just tried to be difficult enough for the Marine Corps to decide that it had had enough of them and would discharge them forthwith. A general discharge was ok with these guys despite the drill instructors' previous warnings that a general discharge would count against them back in the civilian world. I'm sure that there were some dishonorable discharges or BCD's (Bad Conduct Discharges) among this group but our platoon had more important things to occupy our minds.

As our platoon went through one of the chow lines, the CCP types were going though the other line opposite us. Out of nowhere, a Drill Instructor assigned to the CCP appeared and started haranguing one of the CCP recruits for some unknown reason. Maybe we missed the recruit's screw-up but this looked more like an effort by the Drill Instructor to reinforce to the recruit and the group as a whole the reason why he was in the CCP platoon in the first place. Whatever it was, it clearly caught that recruit off guard because he had the classic wide-eyed "WTF" look in his eyes that we had all come to recognize.

Regardless of the reason for the Drill Instructor's actions, it was another object lesson for us and it only reinforced to us what our Drill Instructors had repeated many times to us already: **almost all of us were there because we enlisted; we chose to be there so the best solution for each of us was to**

tough it out and graduate. Now we had seen what the alternative was and it wasn't good.

The snapping-in week turned out to be a blessing in disguise. The close order drills and the nightly education sessions for the less intellectually capable guys in the platoon still took place but the Drill Instructors clearly wanted us to focus on rifle qualification so the usual in-your-face harangues had subsided somewhat. We really didn't know what to expect for the following week and that was actually ok.

Chapter 7

Qualification Week

Monday, October 30.

I remember thinking "why is qualification week going to take a week?" Silly me.

The first half of day one covered the introduction to our rifle coaches, snapping in at the 100-yard line, and setting up our windage and sights before we shot our first rounds. The M-14 could be amazingly accurate if one paid attention to the rifle coaches. Surprisingly, many of us didn't.

Our entire series, approximately 280 of us, were lined up along the entire firing line there at the rifle range. We shot some rounds and moved back to the 300-yard line to repeat the process. This was where we realized why the little spiral 3x5 note pad (AKA the "dope book") was so important. Left and right, up and down - aligning our sights was critical in hitting the bulls-eye downrange regardless of the distance to the target. That was your "dope".

Also critical was the good weather that we had, not only that day but the entire week. We had heard stories of other platoons having to shoot in the rain and wind so we counted this as good fortune in getting past another hurdle on the island.

The next day we worked the "butts" as the target area downrange was referred to. Another series was on the firing line shooting at the targets so Drill Instructors from all four platoons in our series kept an eye on us to make sure that we didn't stick our heads above the berms in front of the targets. As a round would hit the target directly above us, we would look up to confirm that a round hit the target. We would then pull the target down using the pulley that the target was attached to, place a small circular patch over the bullet hole on the target, raise the target back up to its original position above the berm, and momentarily raise and hold a round black metal disc attached to a metal pole over the bullet hole. If the round missed the target altogether (which occasionally happened), we would briefly wave the metal disc in front of the target indicating that the round had completely missed the target. Back on the firing line, the rifle coach assigned to a small number of shooters would track the results and keep score.

The targets at all distances except the 500 yard line were bulls eyes with black centers while the target for the 500-yard line was a larger black silhouette with a small bulls eye in the middle of the silhouette's chest. We didn't make it to the 500-yard line until Tuesday and I wasn't surprised. For a platoon of approximately 70 and a series of approximately 280, it had sunk in on me that all the variables involved explained why qualification took a whole week.

Then we came to Wednesday and they started keeping score. I can't remember at what distance, but somewhere along the way, I started having problems with running sights. This meant that regardless of what the shooter set his dope at, the knob controlling the rifle's sights would start sliding after the first few shots downrange. My rifle coach, a Lance Corporal, was not too understanding and just yelled at me to keep firing. I also noticed that one of our Drill Instructors was standing next to him and did not intervene. Needless to say, I didn't reach a 190 score that day. I just didn't know right then what the consequences were.

To make matters worse that day, some idiot recruit nearby had forgotten a cardinal rule of rifle range etiquette and a **critical object lesson during qualification week: "keep your rifle pointed downrange under ALL circumstances at ALL times**." Hell, even I noticed that he violated the rule.

Unfortunately for him, so did a Drill Instructor and a rifle coach. In a matter of seconds, there was a handful of Drill Instructors, rifle coaches, and a range NCO surrounding the poor idiot. None of us had a good look at who the offender was but we did see him hunching over, then standing upright, then hunching over, again and again from being punched in the gut.

We all knew what was going on because we had all experienced the hunching-over-standing-upright-hunching-over process ourselves. Only later did I realize that one of the reasons that the range personnel and the Drill Instructors surrounded the recruit was to effectively block the view of anyone trying to see what was going on. But at that moment, on that day, none of us cared about that aspect of the incident. We only noted the recruit's mistake and the consequences of that mistake. **Another object lesson: there were almost no exceptions to ALL of the rules here.**

And in this situation, the reason was painfully self-evident. No one could tell immediately if the recruit still had a live round in his rifle, as was the case some years before when a recruit did shoot someone else on the firing line. Whether it was accidental or not, whether there was a live round involved, it was all obviously irrelevant and the Drill Instructors and rifle coaches drilled that point home on that recruit.

While we were on the 300-yard line, another recruit in our platoon, Linebarger, who was a couple of firing boxes down from me, kept missing the bulls-eye as Sergeant Richardson stood over him watching. Richardson started yelling, "You're jerking your shots in there! That's why you're missing the bulls-eye!"

"Jerking" one's shot into the target meant that the shooter was not completely on target through his sights, usually slightly below, and relied upon an ever-so-slight, almost unnoticeable, twitch of the barrel to hit the bulls-eye. Almost unnoticeable to almost anyone else, that is, except for a trained marksmanship instructor like Sgt. Richardson.

Linebarger must have kept jerking his shots because after a few more, Richardson barked at him, "here, give me that finger," pointing at Linebarger's trigger finger. Linebarger held up his finger and Richardson bit the finger hard. How hard? It was hard to tell but I watched Linebarger visibly wince in pain.

Richardson then told him, "There. Now you won't be able to squeeze the trigger hard enough to jerk your rounds in but you'll still be able to fire your weapon the way you're supposed to."

The whole scene lasted less than a minute but for those of us glancing over, the message was clear.

There were three levels of qualification. To the best of my recollection, Marksman, the lowest, was 190-210. Sharpshooter was 210-220 and Expert was 221 up to a max score of 250 although no one ever shot a perfect score that we had heard of. Anything below 190 registered as Unqualified or "UNQ". That term was considerably more derisive than "run drop" because that meant you were a danger to your fellow

Marine in combat and everyone – the Drill Instructors, the PMI, and the rifle coaches - drilled that into us.

Then firing ended for the day and we were marched back to our squad bay. It wasn't hard to see that that our Drill Instructors weren't happy with our overall performance since they were yapping and yelling at us the whole way back to the barracks building.

"You're a fucking embarrassment to the Corps!"

"I wouldn't want your ass next to me in combat!"

And those were tame compared to other insults hurled at us on our way back.

Then it was up the stairwell to the squad bay where the real action started. It was close to evening chow and I, for one, was ready for some food. But that was not to be.

The Drill Instructors briefly huddled in the duty hut while we were standing on line and then re-appeared calling for those who shot expert to step forward. They announced that the Expert group would be allowed to go to evening chow and the rest of us stood there probably thinking "What the hell?" A Drill Instructor yelled for all of the UNQ's to take one step forward, and he promptly and unceremoniously herded them into the head. The third Drill Instructor then called for those who shot Sharpshooter to go over to the nearest window, get down on their knees facing the window and start praying that they would shoot as well the next day.

Those of us still standing on line, those who had shot Marksman, were informed that we were one step above the UNQ's who had just been herded into the head. The order came: "Bends and whoopies! Forever! Begin!"

A few minutes into this, I glanced over at a few of the guys kneeling at the windows, thought about the guys getting to go to evening chow, and remembered that I had running sights that day. If not for that, I would have easily scored higher for the day so as one drill instructor walked past me, I reminded him that he was the one who knew that I had had that problem earlier in the day at the rifle range.

"Sir, the Drill Instructor knows that the private had running sights today."

"I don't give a fuck, Dwyer! Just shut up and keep going!"

Oh, he remembered and he didn't want to hear about it, and so I kept going – Bends and whoopies. For how long? Did it really matter?

After hearing loud thuds coming from the head, those of us still on line doing bends and whoopies then watched the next scene of this whole episode unfold right in front of us. The UNQ's came stumbling out of the head into the squad bay while the Drill Instructors yelled at them to get on their bellies and put their hands behind their backs. They were then ordered to wriggle up and down the entire length of the squad bay floor repeatedly in that position – "like the fucking worms you all are!" - while chanting over and over, "I killed my fellow Marine. Fuck it."

A few of the UNQ's apparently were hurting because we could hear some moans as they wriggled up and down the length of the squad bay floor. This went on for a while and a few of us "Marksmen" engaged in Bends and whoopies were also starting to suffer. I myself looked down in front of me and noticed a puddle of sweat on the floor that had already dripped from my face. How long had it been? Did it really matter? I had already voiced my objection to the

Drill Instructor, such as it was, so I just kept going. If I had learned nothing else from the three mile runs in first phase, it was the object lesson: **"don't give up."**

Still, one of the guys a little further down from me just couldn't do any more bends and whoopies, and collapsed on the floor. The Drill Instructor yelled at a house mouse to go get a bucket of water. Seconds later, the house mouse reappeared with the water. The Drill Instructor took the bucket and threw the water on the recruit. The poor guy rolled over on his side but that was it for him. The Drill Instructor then yelled at another couple guys to carry him into the head while a couple others had to mop up the water on the floor.

While all of this was going on, the "Sharpshooter" group was still on their knees at the windows. From what I could see, a few of them glanced over at the middle of the squad bay at the UNQ's, then quickly turned their heads back towards the windows.

This went on for a while longer until the Drill Instructors apparently decided that they had made their point: there were no excuses for not qualifying on the rifle range. It was time to clean up and get ready for bed. Thank God...

Thursday morning started as though none of the previous evening's events took place. It was off to morning chow, a brief PT session, and then off to the rifle range. As the Drill Instructors had told us, the weather was perfect for shooting. Then they told us that it was "pre-qual day" – a dry run for the real thing on Friday. "So treat today like it's the real thing!"

"Ahhh... repetition," I thought.

And so it began. At the 100-yard line, everyone was given a magazine with 10 rounds to shoot at their individual bulls-eyes down range from the standing off-hand position, then another magazine of 10 rounds from the kneeling position, with a maximum of 5 points for a bulls-eye on each shot in both positions. Proper use of the rifle sling played a role in the standing position so it did help some.

At the 300-yard line, however, the sling made a big difference. Firing the first 10 rounds from the sitting position and the second 10 rounds from the prone position required as little movement of the rifle barrel as possible from the recoil of each shot at that distance. Most if not all of us had learned from the previous days that proper use of the sling was critical and how to make best use of it.

Coming from the 100-yard line, I had dropped only 6 of a possible 100 points and I knew that I was coming up on the positions I was most comfortable with. The rifle coach apparently also realized it because for the first time that week, he was actually helping me and giving encouragement. I dropped 2 of a possible 50 points and then assumed the prone position for the next 10 rounds.

Just as with the previous day, we were given two magazines with 5 rounds each. After finishing the first magazine, we were to remove it, put the second magazine in, and continue firing. Not a big deal until one realized that all that moving around could mess up one's firing position. Regardless of how well one shot that first group, the shooter would need time to adjust after having to switch magazines, all while given the same amount of time for each magazine as the previous day.

The rifle coach had started bragging to his counterparts nearby that I was having an excellent day so far. Then he leaned in and whispered "I'm giving you a magazine with all 10 rounds. Just take a little break between your fifth and sixth shots so they won't notice it."

I started shooting bulls eye after bulls eye, and in the midst of firing those rounds, the rifle coach grabbed my canteen, opened it, and poured the water on the seat of my utility trousers, explaining with a smile to everyone around us that I was on fire and he was just putting the flames out. Apparently, this wasn't the first time that a rifle coach had done this because other rifle coaches nearby chimed in with laughter. I dropped 2 points out of a possible 50, the rifle coach started bragging even more and said "Hell, you might even be the high score on the range today." One of our Drill Instructors reminded the rifle coach that the next day's score is what counted but the Drill Instructor still appeared pretty satisfied with my score up to that point.

On the 500-yard line, we were given just one magazine with the final 10 rounds of the day, all to be fired from the prone position. This time, the target was a silhouette and I knew that I would do well here. I dropped 1 point out of a possible 50 and finished the day with a score of 239 out of 250. Apparently I was tied with someone else for high score on the range for the day but like the Drill Instructor said, Friday was the day that counted.

Qualification Day.

And I was ready. Or so I thought.

After dropping 8 points at the 100 yard line, I proceeded to drop another 8 at the 300. I was already well below my total score for the previous day up to that point with the 500 still to go but I figured that I would drop 2 points at most, maybe only 1. But no – I dropped another 8. I knew what happened, the rifle coach knew what happened, and the Drill Instructors knew what happened. I let the pressure get to me and I simply choked. I finished with a 226 and scored Expert. But it still left a bad taste in my mouth.

Amazingly, though, the entire platoon qualified that day. Out of the corner of my eye during live fire, I noticed that a few guys who were definitely not good with rifles were getting some kind of help from the Drill Instructors or the rifle coaches. Regardless, everyone qualified and the Drill Instructors were satisfied with that.

Earlier, we had all been told that a percentage of us would receive promotions to PFC at graduation. It meant more money but it was also recognition for some accomplishment – high score on the final PFT, high score on the rifle range, or finishing as a squad leader or guide at graduation. I didn't even finish with the platoon high score. At that point, I was mostly focused on just getting through boot camp but held out some hope that I could make it back to being a squad leader.

Chapter 8

Mess Duty Week

The next morning after Qualification Day, the Drill Instructors informed us that our platoon would have mess duty over at the 2nd Battalion mess hall for the following week. We marched over there and were divided into work groups. Some guys would work the chow lines dishing out food to recruits in other platoons, some guys would wash dishes, pots and pans, and some would work in food prep. There were a few other odd jobs, one of which was "Sick Bay Private." The Drill Instructors decided that I would be the Sick Bay Private.

The recruit in that role performed the following tasks:

- Fill enough metal serving pans and trays with the same food being served on the chow line for all three meals. This would be done right after the food prep for each meal had been completed. The Marines in charge of the mess hall would determine how much food to put in the pans and trays.

- Load the food and all the necessary serving utensils, flatware and other needed equipment onto the back of a panel truck at the delivery dock and secure all of it for the ride over to the infirmary.

- Set up everything on tables in an open room at the infirmary and provide assistance to anyone there in line getting their food for that meal. "Anyone" included patients and infirmary staff.

- Gather the pans, trays, and everything else after the meal was over and load it all back onto the panel truck.

- Unload everything at the mess hall delivery dock and help other guys from our platoon take everything inside to the kitchen area where they would clean up from there.

This went on every day for a week. It was tedious and boring but the regular Marines that I worked with in performing these tasks were actually pretty good to me. One thing that I did notice after the first couple days was that some recruits in Sick Bay didn't really appear sick. I wasn't surprised to see it but I was surprised to see more than a few there who appeared to be just malingerers. After a few days, one of the malingerers came up to me after going through the serving line, pulled out a sharp knife and quietly told me his story.

He didn't realize that Parris Island was going to be like this and had tried to get discharged back into civilian life. He didn't care that it would be a general discharge. He just wanted out. When he didn't succeed at that, he decided to injure himself to get sent to Sick Bay and from there he would figure out how to escape the clutches of the Marine Corps, even if he had to cut himself with that knife. I pretty much just nodded and didn't say much of anything to him.

One thing I had learned by then was that if they didn't discharge you under any circumstances, they would simply "recycle" you. Apparently, this fellow also knew that and was looking to create a serious medical issue that would get him the desired outcome of a discharge, again under any circumstances.

During my week as Sick Bay Private, I also had to deal with Navy medical staff assigned to the infirmary. Almost all of them were pretty reasonable except for the Doctor himself, who proved to be a thorn in my side and an arrogant ass on top of that. He gave me grief almost every day about trivial items.

"Who selected the meat and vegetables for this meal?"

"Don't you have anything better for the officers here?"

I had no control over the choice of food and after a couple days of this, I mentioned something to a Lance Corporal at the Mess Hall who was the supervisor back in the kitchen prep area. He replied that I wasn't the first one to notice the arrogant doctor and that the best thing to do was to respect the rank, try not to irritate him, and remember that our platoon was here for only a week.

At the end of the week, I also noticed that the malingerer with the knife was no longer there. I didn't ask what happened to him and no one mentioned him either. I just wanted to put that whole experience with him behind me with as little drama as possible.

Looking back, however, I couldn't help thinking that the Marines working in the Mess Hall had thankless jobs even if their jobs didn't require that much in the way of intelligence.

During that whole week, the Drill Instructors backed off somewhat and Mess Duty week mercifully ended with no problems on the following Saturday. We packed up our sea bags and marched back over to First Battalion and our new squad bay in the First Battalion barracks building.

Chapter 9

Classes and other Minutiae

The following week involved many more classes covering some new subjects but not before we all went to religious services again on Sunday. We soon discovered upon our arrival on the island that different days of the week varied in the tasks from week to week but Sundays always started with services after morning chow. The Drill Instructors separated the platoon into two groups – Catholics (AKA "mackerel snappers") and Protestants. Catholics were herded off to the nearby chapel for Mass while those who self-identified as Protestants, regardless of the denomination, were herded off to some non-denominational service elsewhere. Nobody was given a third choice, so we occasionally noticed a few guys sitting in the pews with us at Mass who were clearly not Catholics. Did we care? Hell, no.

I wasn't a big fan of going to Mass during my time in high school but any reason for a couple hours of peace on ANY day while I was there was worth sitting in a church pew on a Sunday morning.

The following day, a Monday, was taken up for the most part by a mapping class. The instructor was a Gunnery Sergeant, which I found interesting if not odd because up to that point, most of the instructors were Sergeants or a lower rank. But this guy was not dull and actually made the subject interesting. He also started out the class that Monday by reading NFL game results from the previous day out of the local newspaper. He specifically made note of the game between the Miami Dolphins and the New England Patriots which the Dolphins won 52-0. The reason why he mentioned it, as he noted, was because the Dolphins were still undefeated for the season.

The mapping class came in pretty handy the next day because there was an all-day orienteering class held outside. We were supposed to take what we had learned in the mapping class and apply it to the task of finding one's way through any terrain to a destination. As the instructor explained, field operations sometimes didn't go as planned and being able to find our way back to a starting point or the destination was almost as important as the operation itself, whether it was combat, reconnaissance, or something else.

Somewhere along the way that week, they moved me back into a squad leader position. We had also been reminded again by the Drill Instructors that a handful of the guys in the platoon would receive meritorious promotions to PFC upon graduation, a promotion that included more pay every month. Tutoring sessions in the head continued and I began to understand the value of EVERYONE in the platoon doing well in all the necessary aspects of boot camp – passing the PFT, qualifying on the rifle range, passing final inspection. EVERYTHING and EVERYONE. I also realized that there would still be some casualties along the way, whether the individual screwed up sufficiently, dropped out of three mile runs too often, or just became too ill to continue in training for the time being.

One situation brought the stark reality of illness home to me one day when I had noticed that one of the guys who had started out with us at the beginning of forming was no longer in our platoon. The Senior Drill Instructor told us what had happened to him and that the fellow had to spend a few days in the infirmary. As a result, he was set back in the training cycle. How long? The Senior Drill Instructor didn't know but he wanted us to be aware that this could happen to any of us.

Another regular occurrence was the occasional trip to the wash tables outside in between the squad bays on the ground floor. We never used the wash tables because there was a regular laundry schedule in which everyone's dirty laundry would be gathered up in the cloth bags and cinched up with a rope. These would be collected on a given morning after being given advance notice the night before and they were returned to us usually after evening chow.

The wash tables served a different purpose for us. About once a week, the Drill Instructors would allow those among us who smoked cigarettes to go out to the wash tables for 5-10 minutes and squeeze in at

least one smoke. The rest of us were allowed a blessed
period of peace and quiet in the squad bay before the
smokers came back in from their smoke break.

In the meantime, I began to notice that I had a
cough that I couldn't shake. Apparently I was making
some noise at night in the rack because one of the
guys yapped a few times to the Drill Instructors that I
must have had the "fucking" fever. His comments
pissed me off a little but I had already learned another
valuable object lesson: **Keep your comments to
yourself especially when it came to stupid
comments by someone else in the platoon**.

Toward the end of the week, they told us that we
would be getting on a bus that Saturday. Our
destination was Camp Lejeune and the following week
would entail various aspects of infantry training. No
one asked what that meant and with good reason. We
knew that whatever it was, it would be an experience
never to be forgotten.

Chapter 10

Camp Lejeune

Right after morning chow on Saturday, November 18, the entire series all filed on to buses. They had already told us that we were headed to Camp Lejeune and as we headed off base on to the highway, it dawned on me that this was the first I had seen of anything outside Parris Island for two months. TWO MONTHS.

We arrived at Camp Geiger which was part of the Camp Lejeune complex but actually ten miles south of the main base at Camp Lejeune. We didn't know much about it at the time but it was actually closer geographically to MCAS New River, so there was the occasional overhead air traffic from the nearby Air Station. We dropped our sea bags off at our barracks

and immediately went outside to get in formation.
Then we were off to the artillery range.

The rest of the day was pretty much of a blur with
the exception of experiencing a demonstration of a
large caliber artillery piece. It was actually pretty
impressive for someone like me whose only prior
experience with a weapon before Parris Island was a
.22 rifle. The back blast was probably the most
impressive part of the demonstration. And, of course,
there was the usual recruit who wasn't paying
attention and stood directly behind a large weapon
firing a pretty big round.

There was no recoil but there was a pretty good size
back blast to the rear of the artillery. Fortunately, a
Drill Instructor spotted the idiot and shoved him out
of the back blast area before the next round was fired.
We then marched to another area for an introduction
to hand grenades, how to pull the pin, throw them
from the bunker, how to duck immediately after
throwing one. Each of us repeated that process,
mindful of the details demonstrated to us by the range
NCO.

The artillery demonstration and grenade exercise were followed by live-fire training with .45 caliber pistols. There was no qualification exercise and we were informed that if our MOS's required it, we would then go to the pistol range after boot camp for pistol qualification.

Then everyone was issued an M-16 rifle and we went to a nearby range for a little live-fire training on them as well, followed by what felt like a useless exercise in boarding a troop helicopter, flying to a nearby field, and then exiting the helicopter into the field in attack formation. I guess it was worth it for those who would get assigned to the infantry after graduation to experience that drill but for those of us who would be going into other MOS fields, it only felt like another exercise that took up a part of the training day.

On November 19, the Drill Instructors took us out on a five mile forced march with full backpacks. At that point in boot camp, those of us still with the platoon were able to handle that much physical exertion but it was still exhausting. Probably the most interesting part of that day occurred later in the evening when a group of enlisted Marines from a nearby Force Recon platoon there on base decided to swarm through our barracks building, raising hell with the recruit platoons there just for fun. Needless to say, the Drill instructors had experienced this before but still were not happy about the Force Recon incursion.

On November 20, we marched out to the infiltration course – AKA the "snoop and poop" course. Years later, I would see such a scene in movies that I inevitably compared to what our platoon went through that day. All those years later, it made me wonder how much life imitated art or how much art imitated life.

I don't remember how long the course was – it might have been 200 yards for all I could tell – but it was definitely one of the worst 200 yards I have ever survived in my life. There were about 8-10 "lanes" with barbed wire strung across all the lanes for at least half the distance of the course. Everyone was issued all-metal instruments shaped like M-14 rifles, much like the ones that we saw back at Parris Island when we saw the guys standing outside our barracks after their day at "one day mote", and we were instructed to maneuver our way down to the finish line however we could get there. Sometimes it was on our bellies, sometimes on our backs.

They told us before we started that there would be one-pound charges detonated around us as we crawled through the mud under the barbed wire. As I crawled along, at least one of the charges exploded in a nearby bunker that felt like only a few yards away from me. I felt the ground shudder and my ears ring for a few seconds after they exploded and all I could think of at the time was "keep crawling, KEEP CRAWLING!"

While I was trying to crawl through, I saw at least two of our guys get caught in the barbed wire strung a few inches above us across the ditch. Everyone's choice was either crawl on one's back or belly through 8 inches of mud and occasionally bury one's face in the mud to keep moving or crawl on one's forearms and risk getting one's clothes caught in the barbed wire. I saw how poorly it worked for those guys going with the second option. Almost to a man, every one of that group could not get unstuck from the barbed wire for what seemed like the a long time, usually until the next guy behind them in that lane came up behind them and helped free them from the barbed wire.

Crawling on one's back was really the only way to make it through because you could keep the metal rifle replica clutched close to your chest as you inched yourself along in the mud, you could keep the mud off your face and out of your eyes more easily, and you could better avoid getting snagged by the barbed wire a few inches above you. After what seemed forever, that exercise was over and we all assembled back in formation, covered head to toe in mud. Then we marched back to the barracks and cleaned up.

On November 21, we were back out for night time exercises with our M-16's loaded only with blanks and I was as sick as a dog. As we stood in formation, the drill instructor barked out an order to the guide who in turn tilted his head slightly to his left and yelled it out to the squad leaders who were supposed to repeat it to their respective squads. I had made my way back to squad leader but on that day, I had nothing but a raspy voice and it was hard for the Drill Instructor to miss my inability to yell out commands. It only got worse the next day and I could feel myself starting to run a fever.

On Thanksgiving morning, the drill instructors told us that we were basically getting a day off. Up until that point, I had seen a few guys in the platoon get sick enough that they were sent to the base infirmary never to return to our platoon and that usually meant at least another week on the island for them with a new platoon. Until that point, I had determined that regardless of how badly I felt, there was no way in hell that I would raise my hand to get dispatched to the infirmary.

Nevertheless, I was feeling much worse on Thanksgiving morning and decided that I couldn't hold out any longer. I reported to the Drill Instructors with the request to go to sick bay and they immediately ok'ed it. They told me where it was and I high-tailed it over there. It was a short walk but in the cold, I just wanted to get inside the building. The Navy corpsmen checked me in and began to take my vitals.

By then I had a high fever and was feeling pretty crappy in general. They asked if I wanted anything to eat. I replied, "No thanks."

I met with a medic who informed me that if I didn't lose the fever by the next morning, they would keep me over the weekend for observation and treatment. I knew that would lead to another week on the island for me so I asked for extra aspirin for the night and they obliged by giving me plenty to take for the next 12 hours. I was also pretty sure that they knew if I didn't get back to my platoon the next day, I would be set back at least a week in training. Another week at Parris Island was the last thing any recruit wanted and that included me.

I took aspirin throughout the night and when the corpsmen checked me in the morning, I had a normal temperature. I went back to the platoon's squad bay, relieved and thankful. I wasn't out of the woods yet but I had seen enough guys getting dropped back in training because of some illness and I had sworn to myself that I would not let it happen to me so I felt like I had just dodged a huge bullet. We boarded buses the next morning and headed back to Parris Island.

Chapter 11

Third Phase

On Monday, November 27, third phase started. There were still the nightly sessions in the head helping the slower learners with the material in the Marine Corps Handbook and I also learned something. I learned to appreciate what the Drill Instructors were trying to accomplish – graduate properly prepared, basically trained Marines.

After my visit to the infirmary at Camp Geiger the week before, the Drill Instructors decided to replace me as squad leader with someone else. In the meantime, the platoon kept getting better in close order drill. The Drill Instructors noticed it and everyone in the platoon noticed it too.

We knew who our competition would be in the final drill competition, but we were getting more confident with each passing day that we could beat Platoon 1004. And we knew that we were getting a **LOT** better when we were out on the parade deck one day marching past a First Phase platoon. The first phase platoon's Drill Instructor started yapping at them, "Look at them, ladies! That's how good you need to be!"

We LOVED it when we heard that Drill Instructor barking at his platoon. No talking, no eye-balling the area. Eyes straight ahead, moving smartly in unison on every command coming from our Drill Instructor. It felt like we were gaining a sense of purpose as a finely tuned unit performing on the parade deck.

We also had another couple shots at the confidence course. No more coming to attention on the monkey ropes. No more dawdling on the A-frame climb or the "slide for life". We hit the obstacle course one more time as well and that also went fairly smoothly.

Then they threw us what I thought was a useless curveball – the water survival class. Training in Combat Water Survival was supposed to develop a recruit's confidence to stay afloat in the water. All recruits were to pass the minimum required level of

Combat Water Survival-4, which required recruits to perform a variety of water survival and swimming techniques.

But to my eighteen year-old mind, it seemed like a useless exercise. The "swimming techniques" were nothing more than learning to keep afloat while wearing our utilities by using what I thought were questionable movements in the water intended to keep us afloat. I could understand the concept of simulating being overboard at sea while still in combat gear but the whole exercise seemed contrived. Still, this brief exercise did drive home the point of that line in the Marine Corps Hymn: "We will fight our country's battles in the air, on land, and sea."

If one of us was lucky (or unlucky) enough to be stationed aboard a Navy vessel, one would never know if the time would come when one of us would actually end up in the sea. I, for one, considered myself lucky that I never experienced any time aboard a Navy vessel since I would get seasick at the drop of a hat.

We jumped into a pool at what could only be described as an ancient aquatic facility there on base in our full utilities but without our boots on. We were to tread water in a depth of water at least 8 feet deep until they blew the whistle and we could swim over to the side of the pool. This continued for at least 15 to 20 minutes unless, of course, we couldn't keep going. If that was the case, we were to raise our hand, be recognized by one of the Drill Instructors, and swim over to the side of the pool at that point.

Raising one's hand meant that one flunked the water survival test but I determined pretty quickly watching the first couple groups trying to tread water that this would not be a requirement to graduate and get off the island on schedule. For the first time in almost three months, I decided to call it quits on a hunch and, after about 5 minutes, raised my hand. They whistled for me to swim over to the side of the pool and as I climbed out of the pool, I was appropriately harangued by one of our Drill Instructors for not toughing it out. I just stood there and took the verbal abuse before he moved on to the next recruit and another round of yelling in that recruit's face for "not being tough enough."

While third phase continued, a "recycled" recruit joined our platoon. Right before he appeared, the Drill

Instructors gave us some vague warning about him and after he was standing on line with the rest of us, they warned him to behave himself.

A few days later, he was summoned into the duty hut and moments later we could hear thuds against the inside walls of the duty hut. A couple minutes later, he appeared outside the duty hut doorway, looking somewhat disheveled. Those of us close enough to the duty hut could tell that it was obviously him bouncing off the inside walls.

A couple minutes after that, a couple MP's appeared at the far end of the squad bay by the stairwell and walked down towards the duty hut. They each grabbed an arm and hauled him back down the length of the squad bay and out the door to the stair well. And that was the end of him.

That malcontent wasn't the only one to get bounced from our platoon during third phase. One fellow whom the Drill Instructors had nicknamed "Ding Dong" was called up to the front of the squad bay one evening after chow and was immediately taken into the duty hut. After the usual thuds against the wall, they brought him back out into the squad bay into the waiting clutches of a couple MP's who quickly slapped a pair of handcuffs on him and escorted him out the back entrance by the head. We were informed the next day that the guy had committed some crime and tried to escape the local police in his home town by enlisting in the Marine Corps. That was the last that we saw of him, which was just as well since he was a pretty slow learner.

Another platoon drop took place right in front of me one night.

In First Phase, the Drill Instructors began the "Fire Watch" routine for everyone in the platoon. This entailed one guy who walked up and down the length of the squad bay in his utilities and boots after Lights Out from 9 pm until 11 pm. It was his job to keep watch over the squad bay to look out for trouble and to ensure that everyone remained in their racks during the night unless they had to get up to go to the head to relieve themselves. The Fire Watch guys were also responsible for getting "bed wetters" up, out of their racks and into the head to pee.

At 11 pm, the first Fire Watch private woke up the next guy on the schedule and that guy stood watch until 1 am, waking up the next guy on the schedule and so on every two hours until 5 am when one or more of the Drill Instructors woke up and turned on the lights in the squad bay as the signal for everyone to get out of the rack and get ready for that day.

Guys who actually had bedwetting problems were rare but a couple malcontents during the previous couple months had decided that maybe they could get out of Parris Island by pretending to have trouble holding their urine and peeing in their racks during the night, knowing that another one of the other guys would notice it in the morning and report it to the Drill Instructors.

As luck would have it, one guy decided that he had had enough of boot camp and started peeing in his rack at night. We had learned that he was 17 and enlisted after his parents agreed to sign his enlistment forms as an enlistee under the age of 18. Sometime during third phase, he apparently had decided that the way out of Parris Island for him was to pee in his rack during the night. Compounding the problem was that he was on the top rack and his urine dripped down onto his bunkmate in the lower rack. We all wondered why this kid had decided to become a bed wetter after all these weeks and having gone through the worst of boot camp but at that point, we all didn't really give a damn as to his reasons. We wanted to get off the island the right way via graduation and this kid was causing problems.

His bedwetting episodes lasted only a couple nights until the Drill Instructors decided to put him on bedwetting watch. This meant that the Fire Watch privates had to roust him out of his rack every few hours, escort him to the head, observe him peeing at the urinal, then escort him back to his rack and make sure that he got back in bed.

After only a couple nights of this routine, it was my turn on the Fire Watch schedule and I had the 1am-3am shift. Around 2 am, I dutifully went over to his rack and firmly told him to get up and go to the head. Well....he had decided that he had had enough of the every-other-hour trip to the head and told me that he wasn't getting up anymore.

The Drill Instructors were adamant that the Fire Watch privates were not to take "No" for an answer from this kid, so I started to pull him out of his rack onto the squad bay floor. By now, all this noise not only woke up his bunkmate but a few other guys nearby. The kid continued to resist me but fortunately he was 30 pounds lighter and a few inches shorter than me. I grabbed him by one arm and started to drag him from his rack which was about two thirds down the length of the squad bay from the head.

He immediately began to whine loudly and, frankly, I didn't care. We were almost to the entrance to the head when the door to the duty hut opened and out came SSgt Dillon.

Dillon realized almost immediately what had happened, took the kid from me, and dragged him into the head from there while telling me to get back to my Fire Watch duties.

It couldn't have been more than 5 minutes before the MP's arrived and went into the head to take over from Dillon. They dragged the kid out of the squad bay and that was the last we all saw of him.

Occasionally during third phase, the Senior Drill Instructor had night watch in the squad bay. After a particularly hard day, the Senior acknowledged to all of us that night right before lights out as we were all standing on line that we had been through a lot that day. But, he reminded us, we were almost at the end of boot camp and we only had to go through boot camp once while we were in the Marine Corps... unless, of course, we volunteered for Drill Instructor duty.

That, he told us, was almost as hard as boot camp with the implicit exception of no punishment PT. Although he didn't mention it, we also figured that there were also no punches to the solar plexus either during Drill Instructor school.

On numerous occasions during our time up until third phase, some guys received "care packages" of some kind of food. Sometimes, the recipient would experience the hunched-over/stand-upright/hunched-over punishment. A lot of us, including me, had written home, pleading for relatives NOT to send any food of any kind to us. At one point during third phase, however, everyone watched one more episode of "Care Package" punishment. Only this time, I decided that it was worth playing the Drill Instructors' game.

One night at mail call, the Senior Drill Instructor SSgt. Allen read the name on a care package and called out McMakin's name. The entire platoon sang out: "Private McMakin, report to the Senior Drill Instructor!"

McMakin came running up to the front of the squad bay, announced himself to the Senior Drill Instructor and stood at attention as the Senior handed him the care package.

It was a well wrapped, nice sized package and as McMakin opened it, a lot of us watched to see what was in it. He opened the box and it was a container of home-made fudge. SSgt Allen was obviously enjoying the moment and since it was too much fudge for one person to eat, he asked if anyone wanted to help McMakin eat the fudge. After making a quick assessment of the situation and recalling that I had not had any sweets or candy of any kind for the past three months, I immediately raised my hand.

Allen apparently didn't expect anyone to volunteer because he gave me a quizzical look. However, he still barked out, "ok, Dwyer, get up here!"

I scurried up to stand alongside McMakin and SSgt Allen barked at us, "start eating!" And so we started eating the fudge. From where I stood online, I estimated that there was indeed a lot of fudge in the box but I had already taken that into account before I raised my hand.

A couple minutes later, McMakin started to slow down. After all, there was a lot of fudge and we had only made it maybe halfway through the contents. The Senior Drill Instructor then called a house mouse over and told him to bring two canteens of WARM water – not room temperature, but WARM.

I could see where this was going. Allen was going to make us puke and the warm water was intended to push us over the edge. We each chugged down most of our canteens of water and kept eating fudge. After another couple minutes, McMakin couldn't go any further and bent over, obviously not feeling too well.

Meanwhile, I kept going. I hadn't had anything close to this good in three months and figured that I would be ok eating this much fudge at one time. McMakin puked on the floor in front of us and SSgt Allen called a couple of other guys over to help

McMakin clean up the floor. Then he told McMakin to get back on line.

I was still going strong when, after another minute, Allen called for lights out, headed into the duty hut, and everyone climbed into their racks while I stood in the front of the squad bay still eating the fudge. A couple minutes later, Allen came back out while there was still a little fudge to go and barked at me to get in my rack.

I replied, "yes sir", headed over to my rack, and climbed in.

No one mentioned the incident for the remaining time on the island – not the Drill Instructors, not me, not McMakin or anyone else in the platoon. I like to think that Allen realized that I was not trying to show him up, that I simply wanted something like this to eat, even if it looked like too much for most people. And frankly, I wasn't trying to show him up. I just hadn't had anything like that in three months and decided that I could pull it off. And I did.

A few days before the final drill competition, we were marched over to the infirmary one more time and told that we would be getting one more injection in our buttocks. We were told at the infirmary that it was a gamma globulin injection intended to vaccinate us in case we were transferred overseas after boot camp. The Drill Instructors told us that this one might cause a little pain at the injection site but that it would pass by the next day. Not only did it not pass by the next day but out on the parade deck for the next couple days, it was pretty hard for some of us not to limp a little at times from the shot from the pain in the buttocks.

The day before the final drill competition, the Drill Instructors gave us each a round plastic form to fit one of our utility covers on it, and some kind of liquid starch to apply to the cover. The objective was to give the cover a firm shape all around but not so much starch that one could see white stains on the cover after the liquid starch dried. Needless to say, a few of the guys didn't get it right the first time and had to redo it.

We were also told to break out the blousing straps issued at the beginning of boot camp and were shown how to blouse our utility trousers right at the tops of our boots. Blousing straps were miniature elastic bungie cords with even smaller hooks on each end to hook together after wrapping the strap around the top of the boot.

Then we were to tuck the ends of our trousers up under the straps while hiding the straps, smooth out the exterior surface of our utility trousers, and make sure that the blouse did not go above the top of the boot. Doing so would expose the sock on one's foot – a style faux-pas and a huge no-no.

When the day arrived for the final drill comp, there were still about a dozen of us who still felt the effects of the injection. It would have been hard for the judges not to notice it in some of the movements during the competition. As we watched Platoon 1004 perform, we couldn't help but notice that a few members of that platoon were also still feeling the effects. Overall, though, our platoon did not block it out as well as Platoon 1004 did, and they won the competition. To this day, I wonder if this whole episode wasn't another test: "Let's see how they perform when things don't go exactly as planned."

The Company Commander's inspection was next. This time, we were in our Winter Service "A" uniforms

complete with garrison covers (AKA "piss cutters")
and shiny dress shoes, carrying our M-14's. In
retrospect, it was a non-event. We had been through
so much and so many inspections at that point that it
was not as big a deal as they made it out to be.

What should have been a big deal was Elliott's
Beach. This was the final test where we were to show
that we were ready to become Marines. I had heard so
much about it that I was almost not looking forward
to it. We had even heard how they would run everyone
into a shed wearing gas masks, set off some tear gas
inside and make everyone take off their gas masks and
sing the Marine Corps Hymn, all the while breathing
in the tear gas.

A minute later, recruits would come stumbling out
of the shed, coughing and hacking because of the tear
gas, and that would pretty much be the end of that.
But it was not to be. Elliott's Beach was moved inside
that day because of the rainy weather, uncommonly
bad even for Parris Island.

Inside? It was, after all, mid-December but we had
been through much worse. There were all kinds of
tests conducted with the purpose of confirming that

we were ready to become Marines. To me, it was still a big letdown and not that big a deal compared to the previous three months and everything I had heard about Elliott's Beach prior to that. But at that point, I was ready to get the hell off the island.

Since those days, the Marines have replaced Elliott's Beach with the Crucible. Nowadays, according to Marine Corps literature, the Crucible is the final test every recruit must go through to become a Marine. It is designed to test recruits physically, mentally and morally and is supposed to be the defining moment in recruit training. It takes place over 54 hours and includes food and sleep deprivation (only four hours of sleep per night) and approximately 40 miles of marching. The Crucible event pits teams of recruits against a barrage of day and night events requiring every recruit to work together to solve problems, overcome obstacles and help each other along. The event is designed around Core Value Stations, Warrior Stations, the Confidence Course, Reaction Course, and Movement Course as well as other various mentally and physically challenging

events. A final foot march concludes with a Morning
Colors Ceremony and a "Warriors Breakfast."

Needless to say, no one back in 1972 described
Elliott's Beach in those terms and we sure as hell
didn't experience anything close to that. But the whole
experience over the previous three months was still
enough for us.

During Third Phase, the Drill Instructors told us
that some of us were to be interviewed by senior
Marines who had reviewed results of the GCT tests we
took at the beginning of boot camp. In the senior
Marines' questions to me, it wasn't hard to see that
they had bigger plans in mind for me. I knew that I
had pretty much aced all the tests I had taken,
including the German Language test, and I made no
secret about my goal of attending the Defense
Language Institute during the question-and-answer
session with the Staff NCO participating in the
interviews.

Then the moment came. On the night before
graduation, the Senior Drill Instructor gathered us at
the far end of the squad bay, sat us all down on the
floor facing him, and explained what was coming next

after graduation for all of us – general MOS (Military Occupational Specialty) assignments and further school or training to determine more specific MOS's for everyone within a given MOS group. For example, the 4000 MOS group covered all jobs within the Computer Science field – computer operators, applications programmers, systems programmers, data processing officers and so on.

The Senior Drill Instructor got to my name and said, "Dwyer. MOS 4000. Computer Science. Your next duty station is Computer Science School in Quantico."

I immediately raised my hand as I was trained to do when wishing to speak to the Drill Instructors. Allen noticed and growled, "What is it, Dwyer?"

I stood up and replied, "Sir, the private did not sign up for Computer Science School. The private had requested assignment to the Defense Language Institute..."

He barked back at me, "Shut the fuck up, Dwyer. You go where the Marine Corps sends you!"

Just like that, my life was not going in the direction that I wanted but in a totally different and unknown direction and I wasn't happy about it. I didn't especially care for Math or Science, I didn't know a damn thing about computers, and I really didn't want to go to a school for it. I sat back down and wondered what the hell had just happened to my life.

And then it was time for graduation.

Chapter 12

Aftermath, Memories and Other Thoughts

Because of the continuing crappy weather at that time, the graduation ceremonies were held inside at the base theater instead of outside on the parade deck. Other than the fact that I would soon be getting off the island, the whole ceremony was pretty anti-climactic to me.

After graduation, they handed out "yearbooks" as mementos of our time at Parris Island. It was a collection of stock photographs, photos of each individual member of our graduating platoon, and additional photos of our platoon at various points in training during boot camp. Everyone was allowed to order additional yearbooks so I had ordered a couple more for my family in addition to the one that I would receive. Also waiting for a few of us who had ordered them when we first arrived at Parris Island was a set of dress blues. Ever since seeing them at my cousin's wedding, I wanted a set and there they were, boxed up and ready to take home!

Immediately after the graduation ceremony, we marched back over to our squad bay and everyone received their orders for their next duty stations, most of which were schools for everyone's respective assigned MOS group. Some of us departed Parris Island the same way we arrived – on Greyhound buses going to the closest Greyhound terminal for the next leg of the journey, either by bus or plane. Everyone received 10 days leave and it was the individual's responsibility to arrive at the assigned duty station by the date and time specified on the orders.

After my family and I drove back home to Orlando, I was still sounding and feeling pretty crappy so my mother took me to the family doctor for a checkup. His diagnosis was walking pneumonia and bronchitis, which didn't surprise me since I never felt well during

Third Phase after the platoon's return to Parris Island after our week at Camp Lejeune. The doctor gave me a shot of penicillin and a prescription for penicillin tablets, enough to last a week. Thankfully, the antibiotics did their job and within a week, I was close to feeling normal again.

Back at home, my mother also gave me a copy of the Life magazine issue with the article on Marine Basic Training at Parris Island, mostly consisting of a series of photographs with some text accompanying the photos. As I leafed through the pages, I noticed that a few of the photos were of my platoon, including one of our platoon mates crawling through the mud during his one-day motivational platoon visit. He was glancing directly up at the camera as the photographer took his picture so it was impossible not to recognize his face from his graduation photo in the back of the yearbook or from my own memory.

I kept the entire article, including the photos, and to this day, I occasionally take them out of my Parris Island yearbook copy, look at the pictures and a flood of memories from those three months comes rushing back. As it turned out, the photographer had also authored a book a few years later with even more photos and a more detailed description of his time spent there taking all of those photos. I also found it interesting that he went to boot camp there at Parris Island in the late 1960's and, while he did not delve into the physical aspects of Drill Instructors' interactions with recruits, it would be impossible for anyone who went to boot camp there around the same time period not to "read between the lines", and nod knowingly to oneself in acknowledgment of what was really represented there in those photos.

On the Table of Contents page in that same issue, the managing editor added a couple comments after obviously having talked with the author/photographer of the article. According to the editor, the author thought that war was craziness and that the environment at Parris Island in the late 1960's and early 1970's was about as close to a hellish POW camp that a civilized nation would dare to come close to in that day and age. Ironically, though, the magazine editor also commented that the author understood the harsh reasons for Marine boot camp back then and appreciated the results reflected in those recruits graduating from PI back then as well.

The time frame of the 1960's and 1970's was, to put it mildly, a period in our country's history with a lot of racial animosity, violence, intolerance, and bias. The early 1970's was also a period of economic troubles when a lot of enlistees dropped out of high school to enlist in the Marines. If there was any racial bias or animosity prevalent in our platoon, I didn't notice it. Our Senior Drill Instructor was fond of barking at us at least once a week that there was no black or white in his Marine Corps – only Marine Corps green. It should be noted that he was 6'4", lean and muscular, and black. It should also be noted that I never once saw him display any kind of racism or racial bias nor would he tolerate it from anyone in the platoon. We were all "maggots" to him and the other Drill Instructors until the day we all graduated.

To say that our Drill Instructors were all strict but fair would be an accurate and fair statement. One fellow in our platoon, whose last name was Smith, had a tendency to screw up the answers on questions more than the other guys which noticeably irritated the

Drill Instructors. So it was a bit of a surprise that, one day during third phase, he answered a series of questions correctly on Marine Corps ranks and insignia in one of our interminable, almost daily, quiz drills. SSgt Dillon, the questioner that time, immediately blurted out "Out-fucking-standing, Private Smith!!"

Some of us standing online within earshot of them had seen Smith screw up a few times up to that point in training and couldn't help smiling at Dillon's remarks.

Another example occurred during first phase. Every night, everyone had to shower, shave, and then stand online in skivvies and shower shoes for nightly inspection. It wasn't uncommon for a lot of us on any given day to arrive back in the squad bay dirty and sweaty from the day's training schedule. Just as importantly, being clean shaven before getting in the rack for the night was also a requirement.

I was never a big fan of shaving when I was in high school and didn't really appreciate the finer points of a clean-shaven face until one night in First Phase during inspection when Sgt. Michel came up to me, looked me over, and calmly said, "Dwyer, you obviously never paid much attention to shaving because your face still looks like you need to shave. You need to shave against the grain of your beard to do a proper job."

"Yes sir!"

And he moved on to the next guy on line.

When he conducted the nightly inspections the next time, he came up to me, examined my face, nodded, and moved on to the next guy.

To this day, that lesson has stayed with me and I always make sure to have a clean-shaven face with an absolute minimum of stubble on my face when I'm done shaving. Again, that same object lesson has stayed with me over fifty years later: **Pay attention to the details because little things are big things.**

The Drill Instructors could also show that they were human. During third phase, it came about that President Nixon, as part of his wage and price controls in late 1972, decided to freeze all promotions and pay raises in the government, including the military, until sometime in 1973. As it turned out, Sgt.

Michel was due to be promoted shortly after our graduation and he wasn't happy about the freeze. He didn't take it out on the platoon but the Senior Drill Instructor told us one night that Sgt. Michel's promotion was delayed at least for a few months and, as a result, Sgt. Michel wasn't happy about it.

When the Senior Drill Instructor mentioned that, a few of us also noted to ourselves that Michel seemed a little distracted for those couple days and we now understood why. It's also important to note that, back in 1972, the pay scale for members of the military was a fraction of what it is today. For example, the basic monthly pay for a private was $118. Granted, medical care and meals were free, and everyone received a small monthly uniform allowance, but $118 was still a pittance to live on. So it wasn't hard to understand Sgt. Michel's reaction to that news.

Not surprisingly, I came across a blurb on the Internet years later. In the blurb was a reference to a Sergeant Major Donald Michel and I smiled knowingly.

Nowadays, after boot camp graduation, Marines can still take up to 10 days of leave before reporting to the School of Infantry or Marine Combat Training at Camp Geiger, North Carolina, and any follow-on Military Occupational Specialty (MOS) school. Back then, unless one was assigned an Infantry MOS, the next stop was the MOS school as SSgt Allen informed us that night in the squad bay right before graduation.

Not coincidentally, two other guys in the platoon also received orders for Computer Science School. Both had completed at least one year of college and decided to enlist in the Marine Corps. One of them was a perpetual run drop in boot camp and the other one was a pretty good guy, a sort of platoon "admin" who took care of some of the run-of-the-mill paperwork for the Drill Instructors.

At Quantico, in one of our conversations, I remember the platoon admin telling me one story about messing up on some paperwork one time during Third Phase. The Drill Instructors summoned the platoon guide, some guy who had also completed some college, and told the guide to take the "admin" into the head and "educate" him. Translated, the guide was to smack the admin around while in the head to reinforce the concept of "no more screw-ups".

While the guide was of decent size, about 6'2" and 180 pounds, the admin was about the same height and easily another 20 pounds heavier. More importantly, the admin had been a wrestler in high school.

The confrontation in the head ended with the admin smacking the guide around enough to let the guide know that if someone was going to beat up on the admin, it sure as hell wasn't going to be the guide. I smiled when the admin told me the story because I had noticed that the guide was a bit smug in his role and we both wondered if, in fact, the Drill Instructors wanted to teach the guide a lesson about his smugness without kicking him out of his role in Third Phase.

Ironically, one command from the Drill Instructors back then was that recruits were not to gang up or beat on other recruits who were screw-ups. As they told us numerous times, physical punishment was to be meted out by the Drill Instructors, not us. A longtime friend, whom I had asked to review the manuscript for this memoir, asked why our platoon did not take matters into our own hands with the bed wetter in third phase. I replied that the Drill Instructors were upfront early on with our platoon about dishing out physical punishment and that the amazing part about their directive was that in every instance, karma ended up being a bitch for the offending recruit.

Another longtime friend who also went to boot camp at Parris Island a few years after me pointed out to me that First Battalion recruits were a lot closer in proximity to the "powers that be" among the Marine Corps hierarchy on the Island while the Third Battalion recruits were off in the distance on the other side of the Island and therefore not under as much scrutiny by the upper ranks, including the "regimental spies" as our Drill Instructors referred to fellow Marines assigned to keep an eye on training practices across all three training Battalions.

It made sense to me when he told me this but as I said to him, the Drill Instructors knew how to stay out of the spotlight and still "get their point" across to offending recruits. And of course, nothing could prevent Drill Instructors from administering Incentive Physical Training anytime, anywhere that they saw fit.

In early 1976, the word went out from HQMC to improve the candidate pool for Drill Instructor School and, by extension, for Drill Instructor tours at Parris Island and San Diego. At that time, tours lasted a minimum of two years following graduation from Drill Instructor School. Candidates had to be at least at the rank of Corporal and must have scored at least 110 on the General Classification Test (GCT) that every enlisted Marine had taken upon entry to boot camp at either San Diego or Parris Island.

The scuttlebutt had been that recent graduates of the School didn't represent the Marines' best and brightest at training recruits as Marines so the GCT requirements had been increased apparently with the thought that maybe if the candidates scored higher, that must have meant that they would make more intelligent decisions both at School and their subsequent tours of duty on the parade deck.

The logic of the scuttlebutt made sense but it made no difference to me. After being notified by inter-office mail that my name had been added to the list of potential candidates, I was also informed that if I was interested, I would have to extend my enlistment for at least one year in order to complete the school and at least six months on the parade deck at either Recruit Depot.

In early 1976, I was interested only in reaching my date for separation from active duty later that year so I replied back, informing them that I would not extend my enlistment and was not interested in attending Drill Instructor School. All the while, one thought kept coming back to me. During boot camp three years earlier, I remembered our Senior Drill Instructor telling us that boot camp wasn't all that bad since we would only have to go through it once....

...But if we decided later during our time as Marines to become Drill Instructors, the Drill Instructor School was almost as hard as boot camp, just without the constant physical harassment that recruits experienced during boot camp. Those thoughts came back to me when I declined the opportunity to apply for the School. But the thought of me as a Drill Instructor did bring a wry smile to my face. Even my Gunny in our section there at HQMC, whom I had reported to for three years, who himself had served a tour on the parade deck at San Diego as a

Drill Instructor, found the whole idea amusing. He always gave me high marks at review time but he knew that I was not going to extend my enlistment for **ANYTHING.**

ANYTHING included the opportunity to be selected for the MECEP program. MECEP was the Marine Enlisted Commissioning Entry Program, the process by which selected Marines went to college for the next four year taking courses for the major of their choice, still receiving promotions while they went to college, then graduating afterward as a Second Lieutenant and embarking on an as yet undefined six year period of duty that could be completely unrelated to their current MOS.

Again, I had no intention of extending my enlistment despite the fact that the Commanding Officer for our section sat on the MECEP selection board at HQMC and had told me that, given my performance reviews, I was a shoo-in for selection. By then, I was also aware that my current MOS and my three years of experience practically guaranteed me a decent job in Information Technology after my separation from active duty. Also in the back of my head was the requirement for all newly commissioned Marine officers to attend TBS, or The Basic School. After Parris Island and Quantico, I had had my fill of Marine Corps training schools.

In 1980, Edwin McDowell, then a New York Times reporter, wrote a historical novel based largely on his time and experiences in boot camp at Parris Island in the 1950's. Naturally, my curiosity led me to read the book and I came away feeling like McDowell was writing more about someone's experience as a prisoner in a state prison as in the 1950's movie "Cool Hand Luke" with Paul Newman in the leading role.

Boot camp back in the 1950's lasted only 10 weeks and there were documented instances of recruit abuse and deaths at the hands of Drill Instructors. After those incidents came to light, the Marine Corps became more selective in its admission of NCO's to Drill Instructor School and less understanding of Drill Instructors beating up on recruits. Obviously, the punches, profanity, and excessive PT continued but my experience was that our Drill Instructors knew when enough was enough.

Was McDowell's experience the exception or the rule back then in the 1950's? It was hard to say since circumstances and even the environment in 1972 had changed considerably since that time. A lot of the Marine recruits were draftees back in the 1950's, they were probably not thrilled to be at Parris Island to begin with, and I'm sure that feeling was reciprocated sometimes by some Drill Instructors.

Complicating the situation, those guys whose draft lottery numbers in the 1960's and early 1970's were low enough to guarantee being drafted could have done what my older brother did. He was not going to risk begin drafted into the Army or the Marine Corps, and he enlisted in the Air Force after the 1971 draft lottery. Needless to say, those who were drafted into the Marine Corps either didn't think they would get drafted, didn't consider the consequences of their inaction vis-à-vis the draft, or just didn't care what branch of service in which they ended up.

In January, 1973, the federal government ended the draft altogether but the number of young men being drafted in the previous year had also dropped considerably as the nation was transitioning to the all-volunteer military, so almost all of the guys in our platoon had enlisted. It was their choice and their consequences. Regardless, the Marine Corps in 1972 had easily the highest basic training attrition rate of all the branches of the military.

Marine Corps boot camp still had the reputation in 1972, and still has that reputation to this day, for the toughest basic training of all the services. Did this mean that the same practices of the 1950's were still going on at the same rate in 1972? Common sense would say no but the country in 1980 was understandably still going through its post-Vietnam angst and McDowell did choose to write a novel about Parris Island instead of writing a non-fiction memoir like this.

Maybe it was his "novelized" approach to his three months at Parris Island but Kirkus Reviews, the gold standard for book reviews in those days, wasn't too impressed with his effort, calling it "undistinguished." In fact, the review in Kirkus stated "In retrospect, McDowell's diatribe represents a pretty extreme view of Marine Corps boot camp in that time period."

Having read the book, I had a hard time disagreeing with the Kirkus review.

In 1987, the movie "Full Metal Jacket" was released and, of course, I had to go see it shortly after its release. It was advertised as an anti-war movie, with the first half of the movie depicting the "brutal" side of Marine Corps boot camp in the 1960's under an abusive Drill Instructor. As I watched it, it reminded me of small bits of my three months on Parris Island: the occasional nicknames that the Drill Instructors gave to some of the recruits, the consequences of failure to complete the obstacle course, the consequences of being a run drop, the consequences of not answering the Drill Instructors' random questions correctly on details such as rank, insignia, and general orders.

The main theme of the first half of the movie was "consequences", and in the real world of Parris Island in 1972, there were lots of "consequences". There were a lot of small, some not so small, affirming moments for me as I watched that movie: Shooting expert on the rifle range, executing precision movements together as a platoon during close order drill, consistently completing the obstacle course, helping other guys learn all the military minutiae in "head sessions" on so many nights.

There have been a lot of other books published on people's experiences during Marine Corps Boot Camp. Almost all of them were set in times well after 1972.

Closer to home on the "memories" list, my mother would tell me 25 years later, at a wedding anniversary celebration for my wife and me, that she didn't forgive me for years after that moment in my high school senior year for having disappointed her by enlisting in the Marines. After all, she wanted to be able to brag to her friends that her son graduated from the Naval Academy. I remember sitting there across the table in the restaurant having lunch with only her, listening to her, and thinking that whatever my children did or did not accomplish as they got older, I would never have the reaction that my mother had to my decision at the time.

At an event at our daughters' high school in the late 1990's, a fellow student in my oldest daughter's graduating class came over to talk with all of us. He told us that he had enlisted in the Marines and my daughter replied that I had been in the Marine Corps too. He asked what years I was in the Marines and I told him 1972 to 1976.

He replied, "Wow, so you're part of the old Corps!"

I don't remember what I said but I smiled. Afterward, my thoughts went back to my cousin and my grandfather, both of whom had been retired from the Marines, my cousin in the 1990's and my grandfather in the 1920's. I remembered people referring to my grandfather as a "horse Marine" and Marines back in the 1950's as being part of "the old Corps". To be addressed by someone that young as being part of the old Corps struck me as respectful even though I never ever considered myself to be part of "the old Corps".

A few years later, another classmate of a daughter also enlisted in the Marines and we ran into him around town. In our conversation, he used new terms and expressions that I had not heard of during my time at Parris Island and he also mentioned that the Drill Instructors were very conscious of smacking around any recruits, even in the confines of the squad bay, lest they get written up or punished for doing so.

I could only think that times had indeed changed a lot and I couldn't help but wonder if it was a reflection of today's society.

Recently, as my wife and I discussed this book, she reminded me that there were other guys who had gone through boot camp at Parris Island who had said that they did not experience what I had gone through. Nonetheless, I knew that my time there did not adversely affect my outlook on life. To the contrary, those three months and the rest of my four year enlistment taught me the value of sustained hard work, the feeling of pride in one's self after a meaningful accomplishment, and the real meaning of teamwork.

It should also be noted that it isn't my intent to ignore the boot camp at MCRD San Diego or the WM (Woman Marine) training battalion there at Parris Island. I could have probably counted on the fingers of one hand the number of times that our Drill Instructors mentioned San Diego and if they had, most of us probably wouldn't have cared. And we never, ever, saw any WM's while on the Island. We knew that both groups existed but for us, it was always about what was going on right in front of us 24 hours a day and, frankly, we didn't have time to think about much else.

In any large military operation with a long historical record like boot camp at Parris Island, there will always be outliers, those times when some recruit has died or suffered extreme physical cruelty at the hands of a Drill Instructor to the point that it made the news and resulted in appropriate punishment for the Drill Instructor. Everything else for that three month period understandably would fall into a wide spectrum of experiences and memories ranging from "it was a great experience" to "meh, not so bad" to "I'd do anything to get off this Island as soon as possible."

There have been other books published since McDowell's novel. Whether that made a difference in the telling of their stories, I don't know but they're not hard to identify for anyone who wants to research the topic further. It should be noted here that I enlisted in the Marine Corps not out of a sense of duty or service to my country but to escape a dysfunctional, less than desirable home life. Again, 1972 was not a great year to enlist in the military out of patriotism or a sense of duty.

Do I regret my decision to enlist in the Marine Corps? Hell no.

Am I proud of my time in the Marine Corps? Absolutely.

Would I do it again? Yes.

To cite an old aphorism, one's current situation is the sum of experiences and decisions up to that point in one's life and I agree with that sentiment.

There are no agendas in these pages but there is a message. What that message is depends entirely on the reader's perspective and experiences. Nothing more, nothing less.

www.ingramcontent.com/pod-product-compliance
Lightning Source LLC
Chambersburg PA
CBHW071321150726
47997CB00002B/560